This

- You are contempl... ...cess of, a career change, be it plann... ...d.

- You would like to make money out of what you have learned in your career to date.

- You want to understand how to set up a sole practitioner consultancy practice or similar.

- You don't know what you don't know in terms of making the transition successfully.

- You would like to know more about what "good consultancy" looks like.

- You need help in addressing how to sell consultancy services.

- You are keen to achieve "client delight" through your delivery.

- You would welcome someone going on the journey with you.

What people are saying about David Mellor

"Another really useful guide from David Mellor for those looking to grow their businesses. He gives some really practical advice that you can implement straight away. All small business owners should have a copy on their desks!"

Andrew Pullman - People Risk Solutions

"David's a breath of fresh air: he's incisive, direct and perceptive. You'll get no-frills pragmatism with him, as he cuts to the chase, but with the client's interests considered. I couldn't think of a mentor I'd rather have, but David."

Alison Kemp LGSM, MNLP
Director, Switchvision Ltd

"As an organised person, I thought I had factored in everything I needed to get my business off the ground, but there were still things that had not crossed my mind. Both David, and his book offer unemotive and practical input into bite-sized morsels, that you can digest in your own time. You have to learn to believe in yourself and with expert advice on hand, nothing seems insurmountable!"

Georgina Barber
Director, Aesop Company Solutions

"David's enthusiasm for what he does, coupled with wide ranging thought, good ideas, and willingness to help, make him both a catalyst for change and the ideal mentor."

Mark Lauber, Highgate Capital

"David is a consummate mentor - his depth and breadth of experience coupled with a deep understanding of the theory and practice of business both from a corporate perspective and a small business perspective mean that he has learned what works and doesn't work, written it down in plain English and simplified it while still retaining the value of the many years of experience he brings. I have been in business for 20 years, 6 as a business coach and mentor myself - what I learned from David in one hour fundamentally shifted my view of my own business. Buy the book, have a chat - nothing to lose, much to gain..."

Gordon Borer, Exceptional Performers

About the Author

Prior to establishing his own consultancy practice in 2001, David Mellor had a 25-year career in banking with HSBC and Deutsche Bank. Spells in HSBC's UK branch network and in Deutsche's Venture Capital division gave him exposure to the small business market. Since 2001, he has capitalised on this and specialised in mentoring aspiring business owners, launching hundreds of people  on this path, and on occasions persuading people not to do it! Many of the people he has helped have established themselves as sole practitioner consultants. His approach follows a three step process of facilitated discovery:

1. Does the individual have the attitude and mindset to make the adjustment?
2. Does he/she have a proposition that makes sense?
3. What practical tips and hints do they need to help them launch with confidence and achieve success (whatever that means for them) rather than becoming just another casualty?

From Crew To Captain II

A Privateer's Tale

Making the transition from working for a big institution to operating as a sole practitioner consultant

By David Mellor

with original illustrations by James Mellor

www.davidmellormentoring.com

Published by
Filament Publishing Ltd
16, Croydon Road, Waddon, Croydon,
Surrey, CR0 4PA, United Kingdom
Telephone +44 (0)20 8688 2598
Fax +44 (0)20 7183 7186
info@filamentpublishing.com
www.filamentpublishing.com

ISBN 978-1-910125-16-8

Printed by Berforts Information Press
Stevenage & Hastings

For Anne, who continues to support me
on my journey, as she has done since 1974,
who keeps me "grounded" in reality at all times,
and who regularly makes personal
sacrifices for my benefit.

Acknowledgements

Not surprisingly, there are many people who have contributed to this book, directly and indirectly, who deserve to be thanked.

Firstly, I would like to thank Michael Moran and Linda Jackson, who gave me the chance to create my own niche in this area.

Then there is Colin Carnall, a long-time colleague, who has helped me to develop the "sub-niche" of consultancy start-ups in the crucible of a business school environment.

Justine Fisher deserves a special thank-you, because if she hadn't persuaded me to have some video clips shot, I couldn't have helped Ross Moran (who I also thank) with his dissertation, which produced the revelation that I am viewed as "the consultant's consultant"!

I would also like to thank the various "sponsors" who have contributed some highly valuable expert input to the book - Andrew Pullman, Francelle Brims, Ed Simpson, Gordon Westcott and Duncan Hollands.

I am also indebted to a group of people who are all at different stages on this journey and who were prepared to be interviewed about their experience thus far. You will encounter their thoughts and comments as you work your way through the book. So my thanks go to all the people who completed the survey, namely Dave Tod, Paula Sutcliff, Elaine Mason, Colin Charles, Niamh Sandford, Geoff Dodds, Chris Robinson, David Meynell,

Lynne Plater, Martin Hoskins, Jeannette Lichner, Jayne Harrison, Matt Youdale, Julian Sawyer and the mystery person who completed our survey anonymously!

Then there is a whole host of people who have contributed anecdotal evidence; some have contributed on an anonymous basis, whilst others are named in the text.

A number of people took time out to proofread the text for me. I am therefore very grateful to James Mellor, Anne Caborn, Fiona Shafer, Ginette Sibley, Andrew Pullman, and Christian Marshall.

Next to last is my long-suffering PA Vanessa, who has "lived" this process with me for the second time (and she knows there is a third book in the offing!).

Finally, there is my family - Louisa for her constant encouragement and enthusiasm, James for more of his wonderful illustrations, and his social media input, and Anne for her constancy and support in so many ways.

CONTENTS

Foreword

Many people decide to go into business on their own after a successful career in a larger institution. One popular 'destination' for many is that of being a consultant. Most have experienced consultants' work and may have concluded that they were well paid and not doing anything particularly difficult. But there is a good deal of mystery attached to what does or does not make for successful consultancy. Indeed, many of the world's leading consultancy firms have long traded on this mystery because if it were easy, why would they command high consulting fees?

Many enter the world of consulting and do not prosper, finding it possible to earn relatively low fees but difficult to create a sustainable business. This can leave them feeling lonely and disappointed. Away from the corporate support mechanisms or their equivalent in their SME market and the public sector, it can be hard to make an impact. By focusing on the role of the consultant and the effective sale and delivery of consulting services, this book offers a clear framework to assist people plan and carry out the task of launching themselves into a consulting career. The pragmatic approach is based on experience, and sets out to demystify the process.

This book should form the basis of a toolkit for any aspiring consultant. Following the guidance provided will not guarantee success because you must first define the 'unique selling proposition' you bring to market. However, it will advise you on how to do just that, and then assist you in how to leverage that proposition (most effectively). David Mellor has helped many people make this journey to get to what they see as success. I would recommend this book to anyone wishing to embark on this journey. It is as much a process of discovering what you seek to achieve out of the next stage of your career as it is of planning a business start-up. This book will provide support in both these challenges.

Colin Carnall
Director
Cass Executive Education
24th October 2013

Introduction

This book will help you make the transition from working for a big institution to setting up a successful solo venture. I have made this journey, and helped many others do the same.

I want to put the odds in your favour, so that if you decide to follow this path, your venture brings you everything you wish and that you prosper rather than merely survive. As with the original volume of *From Crew to Captain*, published back in 2010, you will find practical tips and hints, all garnered from the University of Life.

The book draws on a broad range of interviews with people who have made or are making this journey, underpinned by anecdotal evidence, from my own experience and that of others.

Together we will look at three important aspects of successful consultancy:

1. The consultant role - what does it look like in practice?
2. Selling consultancy services - how do you go about winning the customers you want?
3. Delivering consultancy services - what can you do to build a viable book of business?

You may be wondering why I decided to put pen to paper again, having written *From Crew to Captain* for an audience of aspiring start-ups. Well, I was mentoring an MBA student at Cass whose dissertation was on the topic of video, and particularly whether video content on the internet was purely for entertainment or whether it could have an underlying business purpose. Coincidentally, I had just had some video clips done for my website, which my "mentee" used in a survey.

The interesting observation arising from his research, for myself at least, was that the majority of people undertaking the survey considered my niche activity to be the role of the "consultant's consultant". So, I decided I had better produce something for that audience, which is a subset of the potential "Crew to Captain" audience - in other words "Crew to Captain" is a broader offering, whereas "A Privateer's Tale" is more tailored.

CHAPTER 1 - A Consultancy Framework

Consultancy Framework

Key Challenges	Consultancy Models	Success Factors
The	*Consultant*	*Role*
Routes to Market	Sales Process	Tendering
Selling	*Consultancy*	*Services*
Retaining High Value Clients	Personal Branding	Do's and Don'ts
Delivering	*Consultancy*	*Services*

Setting the Scene

Business start-up. New Business. Working independently. If any of these phrases apply to you, then please read on. If you have aspirations to build a successful consulting practice, it helps to have some form of framework to ensure that you have a balanced model which will enable you to achieve sustainable profitable growth.

In this opening chapter, I highlight an outline framework to give some context to your planning. I will then go into more detail on each element.

At the highest level, a sensible and pragmatic framework would probably have three components covering:

- The Consultant Role
- Selling Consultancy Services
- Delivering Consultancy Services

Our survey showed that 50% of people are driven by self-determination and desire to work for themselves, as opposed to being "lost" in a big company

In terms of the Consultant Role, we will firstly reflect on the Key Challenges which you would face as a Consultant; we will then move on to consider the different Consultancy Models which you could follow (e.g. subject matter expert, sector expert, change agent…) and decide which is the best one for you; and finally, we will look at the Success Factors which would determine whether you were going to prosper or merely survive. Do you know what you're doing? Do you know how to do it? And how do you know if it's working?

Selling Consultancy Services is often the area which gives most cause for concern, as people are comfortable with their ability to deliver, but less confident that they can win the business in the first place! We start by analysing Routes to Market - how many do you have? We then define a Sales Process, designed to convert strangers into cash in the bank, whilst weeding out potential time wasters and bad debts. Finally, we consider the art of tendering professionally for work.

Our survey showed that the

three main requirements in

terms of external help were:

1. Finance, including tax

2. IT

3. Networks

Delivering Consultancy Services is critical, as this is where your reputation will be won or lost. Retaining High Value Clients is the number one priority. If you create happy clients, not only are they likely to use you again, they will refer others. Personal Branding is also important; is the image you present to the marketplace consistent and coherent, irrespective of where and how you interact with your clients? Lastly, we will look at some Do's and Don'ts, and an appreciation of strategies for success and strategies to avoid is also helpful!

Now we have an outline framework, which we can build on.

The Consultant Role

The Consultant Role is the first of the three constituent components of your consultancy business framework, and we already know we will look at three aspects of this:

- Key Challenges
- Consultancy Models
- Success Factors

Our survey showed the three

biggest challenges were:

1. Positioning/messaging

2. Sales/securing first client

3. Setting up operational
infrastructure

The Key Challenges revolve around you going into consultancy with your eyes wide open, so that you really appreciate what you are getting yourself into.

- One set of challenges is around Credibility; what is it about you and what you know that would lead someone to hire you? Remember, you want people to see you as an investment, and not a cost, so how do you position yourself to achieve this?
- Then there are Behaviours and Attributes; what are the aspects of your behaviour which will help you to be accepted as a source of valuable input?
- And finally there is Lead Generation; do you have a process to turn strangers into customers?

The different Consultancy Models again fall in to three basic categories.

1. Firstly, there is Subject Matter Expert, which helps to address the suspicion of the "jack of all trades". Furthermore, a single product or service cleverly promoted and flexibly applied is likely to command higher fees.
2. Secondly, there is Change Agent, where the consultant has the ability to facilitate either macro or micro change.
3. Finally, there is Trusted Advisor, where the consultant has built sufficient rapport with the client that he becomes the client's "go-to" person on all manner of matters. One of the fundamental questions you need to address is whether you see your role as 100% advisory, 100% operational, or a mix of the two.

Our survey showed

that the biggest

surprise was the length

of time it took to get

some momentum

The third component is Success Factors. What are some of the main areas that you are going to have to focus on if you are going to be successful?

One of the areas is Self-Awareness. How well do you understand yourself? How well do you understand others? Can you adapt your behaviour in order to relate better to others?

Another area is Clarity of Purpose. Are you crystal clear in all your internal planning and all your interaction with the marketplace? What exactly is it that you are offering and is it a compelling proposition?

Price Integrity is also worthy of consideration. Are you genuinely creating the perception that investing in you is a worthwhile decision for the prospect? As a result, are you commanding the fees that you deserve? Or are you operating as a "registered charity"?

We will consider each of these components in Chapter 2.

Selling Consultancy Services

In the first section, I outlined the first of the three components of the framework, namely The Consultant Role. Now I will do the same for the second constituent component, namely Selling Consultancy Services.

Our survey showed the most common change people would make if they were starting again would be investing more money, time and effort in Marketing and Sales

In terms of Selling Consultancy Services, we will firstly reflect on your Routes to Market. We will then move on to consider the Sales Process which you could adopt; and finally we will look at Tendering for competitive bids.

You almost certainly have more than one Route to Market. I suspect there are six main ones. You will have "Route 1" or the Direct route, i.e. you selling direct to the prospect. You will also have an Indirect route, which can be reciprocal i.e. you find potential work for others, and they will be more motivated to look out for potential work for you. Alternatively, you may find "sales agents" who would be prepared to identify work for you, but who would expect some form of payment i.e. they might only do this on a retainer and/or success fee basis.

There might be others with whom you could collaborate to win work you could not win individually; you could enter into formal strategic alliances or joint ventures; and finally there are networks you can join to build your relationships and promote your business.

If we move on to consider the Sales Process, we would start with qualification. How are you going to turn complete strangers into cash in the bank, weeding out potential time-wasters and bad debts along the way? We would also look at Pipeline Management; how will you manage the various targets and prospects who are at different stages of evolution in terms of whether they are going to hire you or not. And then we would look at Asking for the Business; how you would handle the overall sales conversation without feeling awkward about it.

What's been the worst moment?

"Spending a total of over a year working on three separate prospective business partnerships - none of which came to fruition."

The third aspect of sales is Tendering. This has greater relevance if you are pitching for large contracts and/ or pitching as part of a consortium alongside other consultants. We would start by looking at what is often called the "Path to Assent" - how you play to the mindset of the economic buyer i.e. understanding the prospect and his/her world. We would then look at Writing a Bid, and make sure that due attention is paid to bid process requirements and criteria. The third aspect would be Presenting a Bid - how to make best use of the limited time available to reinforce the key aspects of the bid.

These three components of sales will be developed in Chapter 3.

Delivering Consultancy Services

In the previous section, I outlined the second of the three constituent components of the framework, namely Selling Consultancy Services. This time, I will do the same for the third constituent component, namely Delivering Consultancy Services.

In terms of Delivering Consultancy Services, we will firstly concentrate on Retaining High Value Clients. You would then move on to consider the importance of Personal Branding; and finally we will review some of the main "Do's and Don'ts" of the consultancy game.

Retaining High Value Clients is the easiest way to create a stable, predictable baseline cash flow. Your first issue will be ensuring that you follow a Delivery Process which creates happy clients; this in turn will increase the

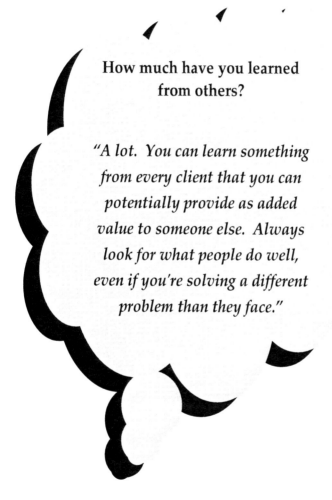

**How much have you learned
from others?**

*"A lot. You can learn something
from every client that you can
potentially provide as added
value to someone else. Always
look for what people do well,
even if you're solving a different
problem than they face."*

likelihood that they come back for more, and refer other potential clients to you. The second issue is Building Trusted Relationships; in many ways, you are selling trust, which, when allied to your relationship-building skills, becomes a very powerful tool. The third issue is having an Appropriate Bag of Tools - toolkits, frameworks and methodologies that enable you to continue to demonstrate that you are adding value (clients have a habit of forgetting the difference you have made!).

The advent of social media has made it very important that you work on your Personal Branding. This needs to be reflected in your approach to sales (being mindful of the Attributes of a good salesperson) as is your networking strategy (which is about building relationships and promoting your business, not selling!). The Coherence of your Image, wherever you are encountered in the real or virtual world, is critical to your success.

Finally, in terms of "Do's and Don't's", it is helpful to keep in mind some of the practical tips and hints which will be value builders in your business as opposed to value destroyers. We will spend some time identifying the 10 Habits of Top Consultants. We will balance this by making sure that you keep an eye out for the 10 Disastrous Strategies. And finally we will consider 10 Time Management Tips, which will help you work smarter, not harder.

As we continue to build our consultancy framework, we will expand on all of these initiatives in Chapter 4.

Our survey showed the top

three worst moments were:

1. *Quiet Periods*

2. *IT/backup failures*

3. *Cash flow pressures*

CHAPTER 2 - The Consultant Role

Key Challenges - Credibility

So far, we have looked at an overall framework for building a successful sole practitioner consultancy. We will now move on to look at the different component parts of the framework in a little more detail.

We began by looking at the three constituent elements of the framework:

- The Consultant Role
- Selling Consultancy Services
- Delivering Consultancy Services

We then considered the three key aspects of the consultancy role:

- Key Challenges
- Consultancy Models
- Success Factors

Drilling down to the next level, three Key Challenges were identified:

- Credibility
- Behaviours and Attributes
- Lead Generation

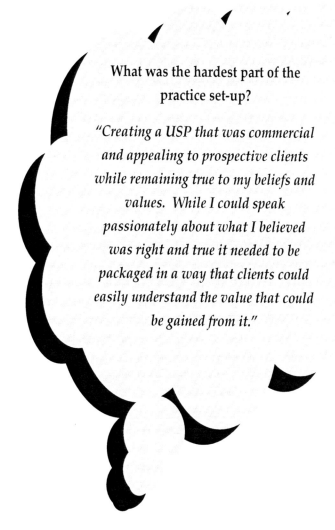

What was the hardest part of the
practice set-up?

*"Creating a USP that was commercial
and appealing to prospective clients
while remaining true to my beliefs and
values. While I could speak
passionately about what I believed
was right and true it needed to be
packaged in a way that clients could
easily understand the value that could
be gained from it."*

In this section, we will consider the first of these - Credibility.

First comes Sector Knowledge. Can you establish your credibility around your knowledge of an industry sector, be it in the public, private or third sector e.g. health, education, biotech, insurance?

Secondly, there is Product or Service Knowledge. Do you have specialist knowledge around a product, service, topic, process?

The third aspect is Publishing. Have you had any research, articles or books published?

Fourthly, there is Commentating. Are you asked to comment on issues or situations, or do you choose to by way of social media output and interaction?

Finally, there is Presenting. Are you invited to speak at networking events, trade fairs, seminars and so on? Or perhaps you are invited to sit on panels?

So, how do you score overall, and are there areas here where you could increase your involvement and thereby enhance your "expert" status?

In the next section, we will look at behaviours. In the meantime, work on your credibility!

Key Challenges - Behaviours and Attributes

Having looked at the first challenge - Credibility - we can now consider Behaviour and Attributes.

I am indebted to Alan Weiss, who explores this topic in some depth in his excellent book, *Getting Started in Consulting*.

He highlights a number of crucial attributes; one of my particular favourites is "Rapid Framing; can you summarise key issues very quickly so the prospect knows that you have listened well and understand his/her problem? Another favourite is "Instantiation"; can you work at practitioner level for the prospect as opposed to espousing theory?

Others which I have personally encountered over the last 15 years or so would include:

- Technical excellence in your chosen field - this will help you to be confident in outlook and have a valuable opinion to express.
- Passion - as with sales, you need to manifest a sense of passion in what you do, and, in this role, in wanting to help others.
- Resilience - you will have to call on your maturity and your tenacity to withstand knock-backs and keep the project on track.
- Commercial savvy - you require this at two levels; understanding from a business acumen standpoint how your business works, and how your client's works as well.

- Influence - can you command an audience, whatever the size, and influence proceedings?
- Reliability - this can range from being responsive at all stages of the process, to being considered as a safe pair of hands who can be trusted not to "drop the ball".
- Authenticity - you are what you say you are, and you subscribe to and live out a professional code of conduct.
- Decisive - your thinking is of a critical nature, and you practise "Ready Aim Fire" as opposed to "Ready Fire Aim".

If you can apply most, if not all, of these attributes, then you can put the odds in your favour that the prospect sees your value and can appreciate the potential benefit of an association with you.

Key Challenges - Lead Generation

On to the last key challenge, namely Lead Generation.

It is very important that you can identify and then work to develop the ingredients necessary to generate the number of leads you will need to achieve your financial targets.

The first of the key ingredients relates to your Sales Process. Do you have a process which quite simply will turn strangers into cash in the bank? You will need to be able to qualify in the business you want and qualify out the business you do not want. Otherwise you run the risk that you expend too much time and energy on potential time-wasters and bad debts.

One additional benefit is that the qualification process should remove all the reasons for not doing the deal, and so asking for the business is a less scary prospect. We will return to consider this in more detail in a later chapter.

The second ingredient is Routes to Market. How many do you have? You will certainly have more than one. They could include:

- Direct - you make the contact yourself.
- Indirect - someone refers the business to you (probably in the hope that you would then feel motivated to return the favour).
- Introducer - someone refers the business to you and you pay them some form of finder's or introducer's fee.
- Partner - you team up with someone else on an appropriate basis so that together you can win business neither of you could win on your own.
- Alliances - this is more of a permanent as opposed to opportunistic approach.
- Networking - you build relationships either at formal networking events or trade fairs/seminars/conferences where you have an opportunity to network.

The third ingredient is Networking itself. How much do you do? Is it the right events and with the right people? Can you create your own network rather than relying on those created by others? Again, we will revisit this in a subsequent chapter.

Consultancy Framework

Key Challenges	Consultancy Models	Success Factors
• *Credibility* • *Behaviours and Attributes* • *Lead Generation*		
Routes to Market	**Sales Process**	**Tendering**
Selling	*Consultancy*	*Services*
Retaining High Value Clients	**Personal Branding**	**Do's and Don'ts**
Delivering	*Consultancy*	*Services*

So, give some thought to where your leads are going to come from, as you may need more than you think to hit an acceptable conversion ratio from lead to client.

Consultancy Models - The Subject Matter Expert (SME)

Having looked at Key Challenges for an early stage consultant, we can move on to look at the first of the potential consultancy models you can adopt, namely Subject Matter Expert.

There is an understandable suspicion and mistrust of the "jack of all trades". One way of countering this is coming up with a single product or service, which can be flexibly applied and cleverly promoted. This in itself can permit a range of approaches:

- Do you want to establish yourself as an "industry guru" who can help a particular sector? I know consultants who have focused their efforts on lawyers, accountants, retail, IT, insurance, and so on.
- Do you want to be perceived as an expert practitioner in a single discipline? Again, I know consultants who have focused on business development/sales, brand building, purchasing, finance etc.
- Or do you want to combine the two e.g. help accountants with business development?

All three of these approaches can be successful. The advantage of creating a "niche" market is that whilst smaller, you can usually command higher fees. If you opt for a more generalist approach, you naturally have a

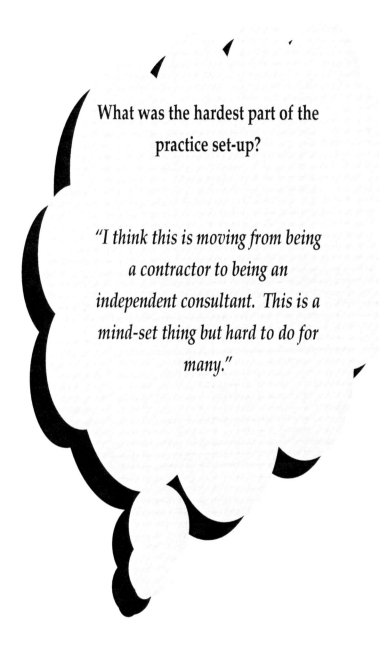

What was the hardest part of the practice set-up?

"I think this is moving from being a contractor to being an independent consultant. This is a mind-set thing but hard to do for many."

much bigger market to exploit, but will probably have to settle for lower fees.

I will suggest to you three ideas to reflect on, based on what I have observed over the last ten years or so:

1. You need to make it easy for your prospects to "get it" - how clearly articulated is your message, as any confusion in the mind of the prospect increases the risk of no sale. I heard a great quote at a leadership workshop: "If there's mist in the pulpit, there's fog in the pews." (Thank you, Mark Fritz)
2. To what extent are your skills portable across industries/sectors? That might determine which approach you take.
3. Will you be 100% advisory (i.e. pure consultant), 100% operational, or a hybrid of the two?

Consultancy Models - The Change Agent

Another potential business model you can adopt is Change Agent.

Organisations are usually well served with people who can "run" operations, often using established processes and procedures. However, they are not necessarily as blessed with people who can bring about effective change, if that is what is required to take the organisation forward. This is where the Change Agent comes in.

Quite often, he or she is operating in a "nether world" between consultancy and contractor, as it is necessary to come up with a plan and then make it happen.

There are five main aspects to the role encountered by the Change Agent:

- Helping management to identify the required action - where is the business, where does it need to be, and what needs to happen to bring about the change and create a successful outcome?
- Helping to create a coherent change plan which will lead to the successful outcome.
- Taking a lead role in the management of implementation risk i.e. how do we deal with all the issues which could be roadblocks to be surmounted on the way?
- Helping with stakeholder management. The number and variety of stakeholders (with varying agendas) will need to be assessed, anticipated, and handled.

- Finally, and most importantly, transferring knowledge in the process. Can the change project be managed in a way that you can leave some form of "legacy" with the client, as to how they could do something similar themselves next time based on what they had learned by doing? This could be a valuable differentiator when you are pitching for a change project.

Consultancy Models - The Trusted Advisor

The third business model option, which may be somewhat aspirational at this stage, is Trusted Advisor.

My good friend Cliff Ferguson of Rainmakers first brought this whole concept to my attention when he showcased the thoughts of James A. Alexander on this topic in one of his newsletters. So, in brief, what were the key points?

Firstly, that Trusted Advisors are more valued than technical experts; their technical expertise is taken as a given. They can build deeper client relationships, provide more complete solutions, and accelerate business development.

Secondly, you can recognise them via a number of characteristics:

- Clients ask for them by name.
- They are sought out for advice that goes beyond their described expertise.
- They maintain relationships that go beyond the technical.

Consultancy Framework

Key Challenges	Consultancy Models	Success Factors
• Credibility • Behaviours and Attributes • Lead Generation	• SME - Subject Matter Expert • Change Agent • Trusted Advisor	
Routes to Market	Sales Process	Tendering
Selling	*Consultancy*	*Services*
Retaining High Value Clients	Personal Branding	Do's and Don'ts
Delivering	*Consultancy*	*Services*

- Importantly for today's world, they have a well-developed personal brand.

Finally, in addition to their technical excellence - as we already covered, this is taken as a "given" - they are first-rate communicators, who are good at seizing the initiative. They always put the client first, and in their dealings, display both confidence and courage. Their business acumen, and their ability to see the big picture, are also strong.

If this is a role to which you seriously aspire, then do not despair if you consider that you fall short of the "Trusted Advisor" standard today. These behaviours, and associated skills, can be worked on and developed over time, so a commitment to personal development makes achieving Trusted Advisor status a real possibility.

Success Factors - Self-Awareness

When establishing the overall framework for a successful sole practitioner consultancy, we cited three Success Factors for people to consider when setting up as a consultant, namely Self-Awareness, Clarity of Purpose, and Price Integrity. We will now consider the first of these in greater detail.

There are some very strong links between understanding yourself better, setting your personal goals, and creating your personal brand. Only then can you come up with a coherent and consistent media and networking strategy. In addition, if you can heighten your appreciation of your own self-awareness, you are in a better position to heighten your awareness of others, thereby relating better to them as a consultant.

Source: PRISM Brain Mapping

I have been using PRISM for some years now, and I have found it to be a very simple and pragmatic way of improving business performance.

So what is PRISM and PRISM Brain Mapping? It is a unique way of identifying people's behaviour preferences based on brain activity. Unlike traditional psychometric instruments, PRISM approaches human behaviour from the perspective of neuroscience, rather than psychological theory. This exciting online tool takes advantage of some of the most up-to-date neuroscience discoveries to provide users with a series of 'maps' which are representations of how their brain prefers to work.

PRISM's reports how not only people's natural or instinctive behaviour preference, but also the extent and the way in which they modify or adapt their preference on occasions to respond to what they see as the demands of specific situations e.g. their job.

The reports also indicate where individuals may be overdoing or not making full use of their preferences. This insight also helps them to understand more about their true potential, as well as what may be hindering them from achieving even higher performance.

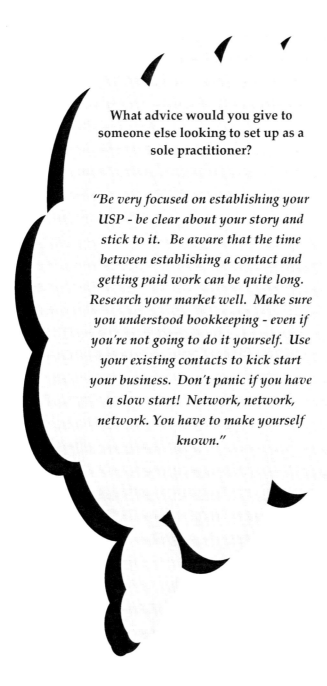

What advice would you give to
someone else looking to set up as a
sole practitioner?

*"Be very focused on establishing your
USP - be clear about your story and
stick to it. Be aware that the time
between establishing a contact and
getting paid work can be quite long.
Research your market well. Make sure
you understood bookkeeping - even if
you're not going to do it yourself. Use
your existing contacts to kick start
your business. Don't panic if you have
a slow start! Network, network,
network. You have to make yourself
known."*

The remarkable complexity of the brain has shown that human beings cannot credibly be divided up into a fixed number of types or groups of people who are unable to act outside of their preferences. PRISM does not, therefore, label people or fit them into 'boxes', nor does it have 'scores', or right or wrong answers. Instead, it provides users with a powerful, graphic explanation for why they approach situations and individuals in different ways.

The brain is the source of all human behaviour. It stores our memories, enables us to feel emotions, gives us our personalities and produces the behaviours that enable us to survive and achieve success. In short, it makes us who we are.

Although genes set boundaries for human behaviour, within these boundaries there is immense room for individual variation. Now, thanks to great advances in brain imaging technology, scientists can watch the brain at work and in great detail and are uncovering many of its secrets.

For all of us, that discovery is really good news. The adult brain can, and does, adapt, develop and change even into old age. This means that education, learning and development takes on a whole new level of importance. Neuroscience has also shown us that people tend to be most motivated and successful when they use and are rewarded for using their own natural, preferred behaviour.

This highlights the importance of matching people with the right jobs - doing those things they enjoy and do best. In simple terms, the better the fit between the person and the job, the better the performance. The best recruitment results come from paying attention to three factors:

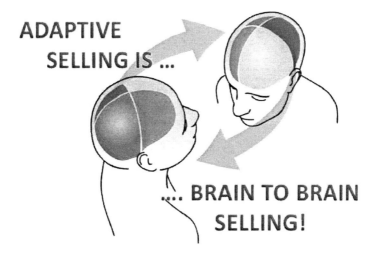

Source: PRISM Brain Mapping

- What the person likes to do most
- What the person does best
- What adds greatest value to the organisation

I have used it for a range of activities with my clients:

- Recruitment
- 360 degree reviews
- Leadership development
- Building high performance teams
- Practising adaptive selling techniques

One of the great benefits is helping people improve their self-awareness, which in turn helps them relate better to others, both within their businesses and outside.

Success Factors - Clarity of Purpose

In all walks of life, clarity of purpose helps.

It is really important that you are clear in your own mind what it is that you are offering, as without that clarity, it will be hard for you to articulate to your prospects what your offering is.

I have set out below 10 questions which you may want to ask yourself. If you can answer these 10 questions in a robust manner, then you are pretty much "good-to-go":

1. What business do I want to be in?
2. What do I want my business to look like five years from now?
3. What key values and principles are going to guide me?
4. Who are my audience?
5. How will I market my offering?
6. How will I run my business?
7. What help do I need to run my business?
8. What are my financial targets?
9. How will I measure my performance?
10. What does my Action Plan look like?

Try capturing your answers to these questions in a one-page plan to keep your approach crisp and concise (see Figure 1 overleaf).

Consultancy Name

Strategy
- Create sell and deliver a distinctive offering around existing intellectual capital and become a trusted advisor within 3 years
- To be first choice in the SME market for business development services....
- ....by building deepening and trusted relationships
- Live out personal code of conduct in the business
- Commit 10% of potentially billable time to giving something back to the community

Marketing and Sales
- Launch website with clear messaging to desired audience and call to action
- Create a social media strategy to drive people to website
- Research and join formal networking group with most relevant attendance mix
- Create own "network" of like-minded people with either overlapping or complementary skills and genuine interest in reciprocity
- Develop a personalised sales process

Operations
- Outsource all infrastructure tasks to quality vendors
- Create a workable delivery process
- Introduce relationship reviews to ensure quality control and increase repeat sales
- Identify quality associates to work with/delegate work to
- Consider using a virtual PA and a mentor

Finance
- Assume day-rate equivalent of £1k
- Assume 12 billable days per month by Q4
- Maintain costs at 20% of turnover
- Create 25% reserve for tax and contingencies
- Maintain liquidity ratio of 1.5:1

KPI's
- Revenue run rate of £9k (Q1) £18k (Q2) £27k (Q3) and £36k (Q4)
- Cost run rate of £1.8k (Q1) £3.6k (Q2) £5.4k (Q3) and £7.2k (Q4)
- 10% quarterly increase in website hits, Linked-In hits and twitter followers
- 10% quarterly increase in newsletter subscribers
- Liquidity ratio of 1.5 to 1

Action Plan
- Incorporate, open bank account, agree legal documentation
- Launch website, launch event, create social media strategy
- Review network, routes to market, and personal development requirements
- Start relationship reviews, review sales and delivery processes
- Analyse product/client profitability, review toolkit, create plan for Year 2

Figure 1

A final thought for you; Michael W. McLaughlin wrote a fantastic article, again commissioned by Cliff Ferguson of Rainmakers, entitled *Creating a Service Offer Your Prospects Can't Refuse*. In the article, he said the following:

"Before most clients buy anything, they expect evidence that shows you can answer three questions:

1. Do you understand the "as-is" state that creates the need for outside help?
2. Do you have a vision of the future in which the current problem becomes a distant memory?
3. What is that path to a brighter future?

If your service offer misses any of these questions, it's a 'dud'."

Worth reflecting on...

Success Factors - Price Integrity

Now it's time to look at Price Integrity.

There are six tips I would invite you to consider in terms of establishing price integrity:

1. Try to price based on value created, not time expended. This is far from easy, but if you don't try, it won't happen! It is very dangerous to assume that there is always a direct correlation between the time you commit and what you are paid.

   Consider the range of activities which you undertake; could some of them be described as "commodity", and some as "value add"? By way of example, a sole practitioner accountant probably has a range of activities which could be described as commodity (preparing a set of accounts), but may also have some activities where he is genuinely making a difference (devising and implementing an efficient tax management strategy). These probably deserve different levels of reward.

2. Consider pricing options. Does your business lend itself to Day Rate, Fixed Fee, Performance Related, or a hybrid of these? I have used all of these at different times.

3. Structure proposals on a modular basis. The reason for this is you can then trade time for money, and not just face having to concede i.e. if the client balks at the price, you can just take a module out and bring the price down accordingly.

What was your biggest surprise?

"The length of time from first meeting until it turns into actual work."

4. Know your worth. If you are offering a "Rolls Royce" service, the prospect will be confused if you are offering a bargain basement price. You need to stay in line with the market, and you need to match your pricing to your overall strategy - low-cost offering/ niche offering/differentiated offering - with the latter two representing the best opportunities to price at the top of the market.

5. Be prepared to take a degree of risk - this brings us back to the performance-related aspect. I have on occasions done work where I have offered the prospect a choice between a full day rate and a lower day rate with a performance "kicker" if a target increase in pre-tax profit is achieved by a certain date (and on a formula agreed with the client's accountant so there can be no "misunderstandings").

6. Be prepared to walk away. If you sense that you are viewed as a cost as opposed to an investment then, unless your model is to be a low-cost provider, or there is some form of ulterior motive, you should think long and hard before agreeing to undertake work at an unsatisfactory fee level.

Consultancy Framework

Key Challenges	Consultancy Models	Success Factors
• Credibility • Behaviours and Attributes • Lead Generation	• SME - Subject Matter Expert • Change Agent • Trusted Advisor	• Self-Awareness • Clarity of Purpose • Price Integrity
Routes to Market	Sales Process	Tendering
Selling	*Consultancy*	*Services*
Retaining High Value Clients	Personal Branding	Do's and Don'ts
Delivering	*Consultancy*	*Services*

CHAPTER 3 - Selling Consultancy Services

Routes to Market - Direct

When considering sales, one of the first things to think about is Routes to Market; how many do you have? We all have more than one; it's just a case of figuring out just how many. In this section, we will deal with the most obvious one, what I call "direct".

What would classify a sale as direct? Several factors:

1. You identify the potential client as a prospect in the first place. You have assessed his or her potential interest in your offering based on sector, size, and location, and so on...
2. You make direct contact with the client, by one of the following mechanisms:

   • Networking (either at a formal networking group, or opportunistically at a seminar, conference, trade fair etc.)
   • Cold approach - letter, email, phone call...
   • Social media - an initial relationship with the prospect is built via one or more of the sites - LinkedIn, Twitter, Facebook
   • Subscription - the prospect registers on your website to receive further information prompted by blogs, newsletters, and other articles

3. You handle the sales process at all stages with little or no intervention from anybody else on your behalf.
4. Your "cost of sales", or client acquisition cost, relates to your efforts and initiatives, no-one else's e.g. networking subscription fees, direct marketing

campaign, travel, entertainment. One notable exception could be if you are retaining someone else to create marketing collateral for you i.e. a freelance copywriter.

So, in the case of this route to market, you are succeeding or failing based on your own lead generation efforts.

Routes to Market - Indirect

Indirect routes will now feature in your sales planning. Reciprocal is the first type of indirect route. This is where you identify people you like and trust, and who are ready, willing and able to refer qualified opportunities to you, in the expectation that you would be equally prepared to do the same for them. In this type of arrangement, which is informal, no money changes hands. You are much better off having a handful of these types of relationships that really deliver, rather than a vast number that deliver nothing and effectively waste your time.

The second type is fee-based, preferably on a mutual as opposed to one-way basis. This in effect means that the originator of the opportunity pays the other a fee for sourcing the work. This can be a significant source of business for you, but you need to bear a few things in mind:

- There has to be a platform of mutual trust to begin with, otherwise you have nothing to build on.
- The arrangement has to be documented.
- The fee split has to be sufficiently interesting to motivate people to spend time finding work for you

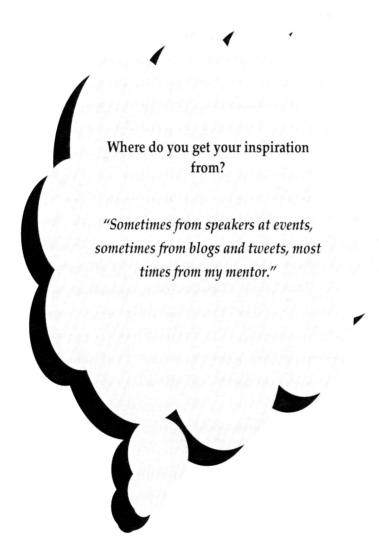

Where do you get your inspiration from?

"Sometimes from speakers at events, sometimes from blogs and tweets, most times from my mentor."

(and vice versa, of course!). I would suggest 10% of revenue if it is a straight referral, maybe up to 20% if the other party is actively involved in the sales process and actually helps you close the deal.

- The duration of the agreement should probably be finite - again, I would suggest 12 months from when the works starts; in year 2, you are in all likelihood being retained on your own efforts.
- There needs to be transparency and honesty at all times between you and the other party in terms of work undertaken and fees earned.

So, in the case of this route to market, you are succeeding or failing based on your ability to build relationships with others who will channel meaningful and relevant opportunities to you.

Routes to Market – Other

Having looked at "direct" and "indirect" routes to market, we will take a slightly different tack and consider other routes.

Let's consider two extremes of activity for a moment. At one end of the spectrum, there are assignments you are perfectly capable of winning and delivering on your own. If you can "fill your boots" using either the direct or indirect routes, then fine; long may that continue! At the other end of the spectrum, you may be able to act as an associate of a much bigger institution, securing work which may often be otherwise beyond you as it requires a significant delivery team of which you are one member. Normally nice work, if you can get it; you may have to operate at a lower pay rate than you could secure independently, but you have normally had no client acquisition cost; you just have to turn up and do the work.

If you find that these two extremes are not sufficient to fill your diary, then there are a couple more that you can consider.

Firstly, you can try to identify people who do similar things to you, and where, if you teamed up, you could win work none of you could win on your own. By way of example, I teamed up with two other consultants and we ran a six-module leadership development programme, delivering two modules each.

Consultancy Framework

Key Challenges	Consultancy Models	Success Factors
• Credibility • Behaviours and Attributes • Lead Generation	• SME - Subject Matter Expert • Change Agent • Trusted Advisor	• Self-Awareness • Clarity of Purpose • Price Integrity
Routes to Market	**Sales Process**	**Tendering**
• Direct • Indirect • Other		
Retaining High Value Clients	**Personal Branding**	**Do's and Don'ts**
Delivering	*Consultancy*	*Services*

Secondly, you can try to identify other professional firms where you can develop the reciprocity approach we talked about under "indirect" routes. In addition to referring prospects to each other, you could run joint events/seminars/campaigns on linked or related topics. I have run a number of seminars with lawyers and accountants which have been well received. One which worked particularly well was a breakfast seminar which I ran with a firm of lawyers where we looked through a couple of case studies from our own experiences of real-life examples of boardroom dilemmas, and challenged the group to consider what they would do if they were a Non-Executive Director of the business. It was great fun (I have to confess, we injected a little bit of "Gallows Humour" for dramatic effect!), but some good learning points were uncovered.

In conclusion, do broaden your thinking to consider alternative routes to market. Some will work better for you than others, but unless you explore them all, you will never know which ones.

Sales Process - Qualification

Having a Sales Qualification Process is very important. It has a number of purposes:

1. It will help you to turn strangers into cash in the bank.
2. You can profile the clients you want (as opposed to merely accepting those who find you).
3. You can weed out potential time-wasters.
4. You can weed out bad debts.

I have included the one I use in my consulting work just to give you an idea (see Figure 2 overleaf).

The sorts of things you would want to cover in your sales qualification would include:

- Source of lead or referral. Where did the opportunity come from? Is it from a trusted source who you know would only pass you a qualified opportunity, or is it a less trusted resource that may be passing you a problem?
- Potential size of transaction. If it's huge, don't just rub your hands together with delight. Think about whether you can actually deliver or whether you would embarrass yourself if you could not cope. If it's tiny, don't decline out of hand. Think about whether you are being tested, and if you do a good job will you get something more substantial down the line.
- Size of company. In days gone by, the larger the company, the more likely they would be there to pay you when you finish the work, but the current economic climate has indicated this is not necessarily

Sales Process - Figure 2

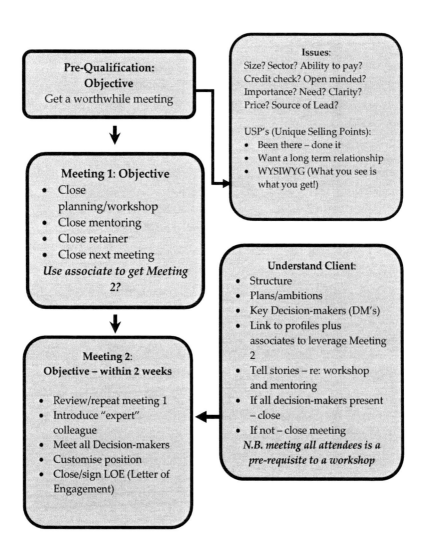

the case. With smaller businesses, you may want to check their ability to pay. There are credit checks you can do by using agencies that have access to the same databases that the banks have; they normally do debt recovery also! This is obviously for business to business. The credit cycle with consumers is obviously a great deal shorter.

- Identification of decision maker. Nothing is more frustrating than pitching to the wrong person. If you have identified the decision maker, great! If not, can you positively influence the person who is representing your interests to give a good account of your proposition? Make sure you understand the decision-making process.

- Identification of budget. Find out if your prospect has a budget. If the prospect has not allocated a budget, then how serious are they?

- Clarity of requirement. Are you clear in your mind what the client wants and whether you can deliver it?

- Urgency of requirement. Is this mission critical for them or not? If it's not, then if they get busy, could it cease to be important?

- Finally, why are they talking to you? What has prompted them to contact you? Are they serious about getting a quote, or are you just there to make up the numbers? If that is the case, you do not want to waste your time if there is no chance to win the business.

If you stop and think for a moment, you can begin to appreciate that if you follow this process every time, you will have eliminated all the reasons for not wanting to sell to the prospect; equally, the prospect has eliminated

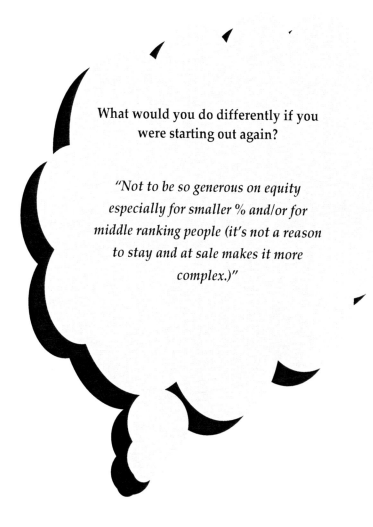

What would you do differently if you
were starting out again?

*"Not to be so generous on equity
especially for smaller % and/or for
middle ranking people (it's not a reason
to stay and at sale makes it more
complex.)"*

all the reasons for not wanting to buy from you! So, he or she is going to be surprised if you don't ask for the business – but we'll come back to that later.

Sales Process - Pipeline Management

The first aspect to consider is the sales pipeline itself. As you gather names, you will end up with a range of prospects at different stages of evolution. It will help you if you can track each prospect at each stage so that you keep it moving, hopefully with some momentum, in the right direction. The typical stages you would track (with potential likelihood of success) could include:

1. Target = 0%
2. Contact established = 10%
3. Positive meeting = 20%
4. Tender submitted = 30%
5. Negotiations/discussions = 50%
6. Verbal OK or email = 75%
7. Purchase order/contract = 100%

By way of example, if you have moved a target to stage five, as is the case with Prospect E in Figure 3 overleaf, you may well believe you have a 50-50 chance of success, so you allocate a 50% factor to the value of the work i.e. a £3,000 contract would be ascribed a value of £1,500 at that stage. If you do this for your entire pipeline list of names, you can not only track status and action required, but ascribe a figure to your potential future cash flow.

The second aspect is conversion ratios (see Figure 4). It is helpful to set and then, with experience, adjust how

many targets you need to pursue to get the number of clients you need i.e. how many "targets" do you need to have at stage one to get the number of clients you need making it to stage seven.

So you need to think about conversion ratios. What this is assuming is that to hit your sales target for the year you, need 10 clients. The subsequent assumptions might be the following.

You can win one in three proposals, so you have to do 30 proposals; once in every five meetings, a prospect will ask you to submit a tender or a proposal, so you have to do 150 meetings; and finally out of every 10 people that you contact, one agrees to meet with you. If you then flip it the other way, if you contact 1,500 people either at a networking meeting or by phone, letter or email, then 150 will agree to meet you, of which 30 will allow you to submit a proposal, and 10 will be won.

You now have a rough estimate of how hard you will need to work to get the number of clients you need. In Year 2, it should be more scientific as you will have a year's data. You will have an idea of how much work you would need to do at the front end to get the requisite number of clients. Please note that these ratios are for illustration only.

The third aspect is having some mechanisms for dealing with sales that seem stuck somewhere in the process. Andrew Sobel, in yet another article commissioned by Cliff Ferguson called *What to Do when the Sale Stalls*, talks about "6 preconditions to create a buyer":

Pipeline - Figure 3

Pipeline (Source: Viridian Corporate Finance Ltd)			
Name	Stage	Contract size (est.)	Value
A	1	1000	0
B	2	2000	200
C	3	5000	1000
D	4	1200	400
E	5	3000	1500
F	6	10000	7500
G	7	1000	1000
H	1	500	0
I	3	2000	400
J	4	1500	500
K	5	4000	2000
L	2	1000	100
M	2	5000	1000
N	4	3000	1000
		40200	16600

Assumptions

1. Prospect = 0%
2. Contact established = 10%
3. Positive meeting = 20%
4. Tender Submitted = 30%
5. Negotiations/discussions = 50%
6. Verbal o.k. or email = 75%
7. Purchase order/contract = 100%

Activity Plan / Conversion Ratios
Figure 4

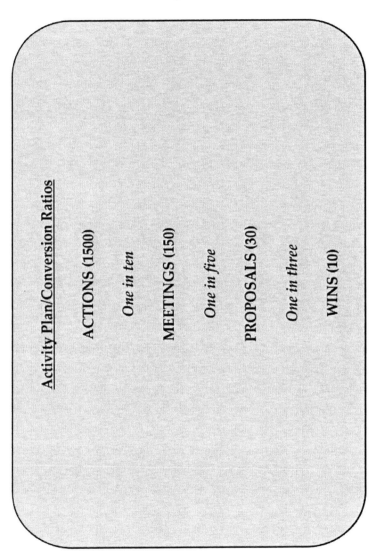

Activity Plan/Conversion Ratios

ACTIONS (1500)

One in ten

MEETINGS (150)

One in five

PROPOSALS (30)

One in three

WINS (10)

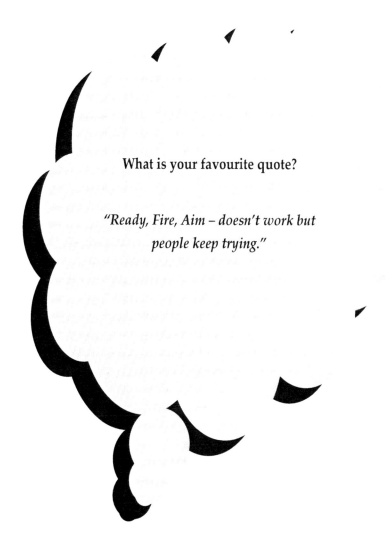

What is your favourite quote?

"Ready, Fire, Aim – doesn't work but people keep trying."

1. The client perceives a problem or opportunity that is significant in size and importance.
2. The client has a healthy dissatisfaction with the rate of change.
3. The client believes there is a material lack of internal resource and/or expertise.
4. The client trusts that you can do it.
5. The executive sponsor feels that the right stakeholders have all been aligned around retaining you and utilising your approach.
6. They can see tangible next steps to move forward.

If any of these preconditions are missing, then the sales process will stall. So worth checking back with the potential clients to gauge how present these 6 preconditions are.

Sales Process - Asking for the Business

It's not everyone that finds asking for business easy.

Let's start by looking at some of the things that crop up in sales meetings.

1. Remember to differentiate between the features (what it is) and the benefits (what's in it for the buyer) of your offering.
2. If you are asked what your USP (Unique Selling Point or Unique Selling Proposition) is, make sure you have a response. Silence will not help your cause.
3. If you are asked for proof that you can do what you say are offering, ensure you have some options up your sleeve e.g. qualifications, case studies, testimonials. The crucial issue is to "de-risk" the decision from the buyer's perspective.

Secondly, when discussing price, try to have two approaches in mind; if it is a straightforward requirement, quote the price and then stay silent - you don't need to justify it. On the other hand, if it is complicated, merely state that you will go away, work it out, and have a firm figure to the prospect within a certain period.

Whatever you do, avoid thinking out loud in front of the prospect - a rocky road to losing the sale. If you get pushback on price, think about whether you can trade time and not money e.g. if you have offered a "modular" solution then take out a couple of modules if you are prepared to lower the price.

Consultancy Framework

Key Challenges	Consultancy Models	Success Factors
• Credibility • Behaviours and Attributes • Lead Generation	• SME - Subject Matter Expert • Change Agent • Trusted Advisor	• Self-Awareness • Clarity of Purpose • Price Integrity
Routes to Market	**Sales Process**	**Tendering**
• Direct • Indirect • Other	• Qualification • Pipeline Management • Asking for the Business	
Retaining High Value Clients	**Personal Branding**	**Do's and Don'ts**
Delivering	*Consultancy*	*Services*

Finally, develop a few ways of asking for the business with which you are comfortable. A couple of examples that have worked well for me are:

1. The "alternative close". Would you like to start this month or next month (the "will you buy it or will you buy it" approach)?
2. The "summary close". You (the client) have identified several benefits which would arise from doing this work (repeat them); should we therefore put a date in the diary to make a start?

In a perfect world, you create a situation where the prospect wants to buy from you rather than you sell to them, but the world is not perfect, so you need a few tips and hints which you can employ.

Tendering - Path to Assent

I am indebted to Tom Lambert, author of *High Income Consultancy*, who inspired this little section with his concept of Path to Assent. It is time to talk about how to get the best out of the tendering process, and how to win an unfair share of competitive bids, which sometimes come into play even on small assignments.

Understanding the prospect, and playing to his or her mindset, is critical if you are going to be successful. We will talk about writing and presenting bids in due course, but at this stage it is helpful to focus on the preparatory stage i.e. preparing for an exploratory or fact-finding meeting.

It will be helpful to keep in mind the attitude and mindset of the prospect, and whilst each situation will inevitably differ, there are certain steps on the "path to assent" which will apply most of the time:

1. It will be difficult, particularly if prospects don't know you very well already (which may sometimes be the case), to even start making progress if they feel they are not being treated with the respect they deserve.
2. Coupled with this is an acknowledgement that they know a good deal about their business, and that their accumulated experience counts in determining a range of possible solutions and associated outcomes.
3. If these two potential barriers on the path can be passed, you can move on to explain to them that you can help them achieve a result they could not achieve without you.

Our survey showed that 70% of practitioners had to adapt their original proposition in one way or the other

4. If you can successfully convey that this is indeed a real possibility, you can then run through your preferred solution (by the way, giving them choices can sometimes be quite a powerful tactic) and explore with them the likely outcome and the difference it will have made.

You will not necessarily complete all these stages at one meeting, but it helps to keep them in mind as you build your picture of the prospect and his or her world.

The evolution of the relationship you are trying to build with the prospect - and remember, people buy people before they buy a product or service - may look something like this:

- A meeting is agreed.
- A relationship is established.
- A conceptual agreement on outcomes is reached - this will include objectives, how to measure progress, and the value to the buyer's business.
- A proposal is crafted and presented.

If you keep this evolution in mind, it may help you to come up with an effective tendering process capable of successful replication.

Tendering - Writing a Bid

It is worthwhile spending time crafting a quality bid or proposal, as this will be the reference point on your offering when you are not in the prospect's presence. I was very fortunate a few years ago to attend a workshop on Successfully Consultancy, hosted by the Institute of Directors, at which Harold Lewis shared some top tips on crafting a bid, which included:

1. Do your research
2. Weigh up the competitive opportunity
3. Read tender documents thoroughly
4. Plan the bid writing process
5. Follow all clients' instructions
6. Treat policy statements seriously
7. Focus on client priorities and your distinctive value
8. Justify everything
9. Be honest and realistic
10. Establish clarity

I would like to add some further flavour to one of these tips, and then add one more.

Our survey showed that over 50% of those interviewed felt that the greatest sense of fulfilment came from winning a new client

So, firstly, preparation in general, and research in particular.

It pays to take every opportunity when you can interact with the potential client to glean more information and context. People buy people before they buy the service, so these are good opportunities to build empathy and rapport.

Put yourself in the buyer's shoes; what's going on in their world? If you can ask questions that lead to outcome-based objectives, so much the better. In addition, make sure you study their website, and any social media activity in which they engage. Finally, look for any recent press coverage, which might give clues on what is going on in the business.

And the additional point. In terms of stakeholder management, do keep in mind that there may be more than one party involved in the recommendation/decision, and that they may have different agendas.

If you can, try to weave in something that plays to these different audiences, their issues and concerns, and the way in which they like to receive information. One note of caution - a common problem is giving the prospect a clear outline of what you plan to do so they can then embark without your assistance.

Tendering - Presenting a Bid

Presenting a bid needs as much attention whether it is "one to one" or to a panel.

Your written bid has done its job, and you have been invited to present it in person. The first rule is, whatever you do, don't "wing it"; it will very rarely work for you. The second rule is there is only one rule (thank you, Monty Python!).

First, let's consider a few general tips about how to deal with the audience:

1. Plan your presentation from the listener's perspective.
2. Create for your listener an awareness of the need to act now.
3. Maintain and build the listener's interest.
4. Tell the listener all they need to know about your services as far as they are relevant to him/her.
5. Explain the benefits of your service.
6. Check to ensure you have not lost the listener's attention.
7. Be prepared for questions, and make sure you have robust answers for the questions you would least like to be asked.
8. Don't use jargon.
9. Have a component in your presentation which makes you and your bid distinctive, but resist the temptation to give them the wherewithal to do the job without you.
10. Don't forget that if you have more than one listener, they may be looking for different things from you,

What's given you your biggest "buzz"?

"Winning the very first piece of business. That memory will stay with me forever."

based on their behaviour preferences and their respective roles in the business.
11. Be authentic, and be yourself.

I would like to finish with a couple of thoughts on how you structure your presentation.

Firstly, keep it as short as you can and focus on the essentials. What are the key issues you need to highlight from your proposal, and don't spend much time telling them how good you are; they appreciate that or you wouldn't have been shortlisted.

Secondly, make sure the proposal has a structure, so that you lead the listener through to a positive decision-inducing position (i.e. acceptance). Items you may want to reference could include:

- The objectives of the assignment.
- Measures of success (e.g. indicators of progress being made).
- Expressions of value (what improvements and enhancements can be expected; in other words, what success could look like).
- Methodologies and options (how you will address the issues).
- Timing (so both party's expectations are managed).
- Joint accountabilities (who is responsible for what).
- Key terms and conditions.

Consultancy Framework

Key Challenges	Consultancy Models	Success Factors
• Credibility • Behaviours and Attributes • Lead Generation	• SME - Subject Matter Expert • Change Agent • Trusted Advisor	• Self-Awareness • Clarity of Purpose • Price Integrity
Routes to Market	**Sales Process**	**Tendering**
• Direct • Indirect • Other	• Qualification • Pipeline Management • Asking for the Business	• Path to Assent • Writing a Bid • Presenting a Bid
Retaining High Value Clients	**Personal Branding**	**Do's and Don'ts**
Delivering	*Consultancy*	*Services*

Above all, just try to be your natural self. If you try to be someone you are not, it will probably undermine your performance. So, let them see the authentic you. We will shortly consider personal branding, of which this is a core element, along with;

- Credibility
- Constancy
- Consistency

CHAPTER 4 - Delivering Consultancy Services

Retaining High Value Clients – Delivery Process

We are going to look at Retaining High Value Clients, which is one of the key aspects of the Delivery Process. We need to bear in mind that a sound delivery process has twin purposes; to create happy clients who a) come back for more and b) refer other people to you. The accepted wisdom is that a happy client is worth two quality referrals, so it makes perfect sense to exploit this. Figure 5 is the process I use in my work.

Two of the most important goals arising out of your process are:

- Seeking repeat business at the right moment (ideally when the client is at his/her happiest)
- Seeking referrals at the same time

To these, you could add a third goal, namely:

- Working to a process to ensure there is no deviation from the core assignment, managing client expectations all the way, with checkpoint reviews.

Delivery Process (Figure 5)

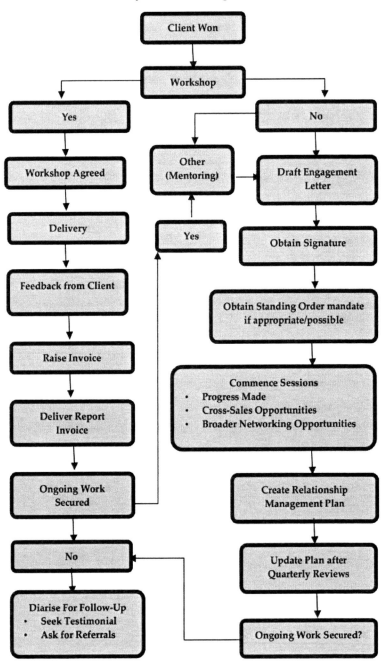

Why is this third goal important? Well, it is dangerous to assume that the client is happy, and that he/she understands and appreciates the difference you are making. In addition, you do not want to fall foul of an industry disease known as "scope creep", where all sorts of little bits and pieces get tacked on to the work, not necessarily with an increase in fees, which risk the delivery deadline being compromised.

A couple of other factors to bear in mind:

1. If you are going to require support in order to deliver the work, make sure you only use top quality associates; to do otherwise is courting disaster.
2. Keep a close eye on outputs and time, so that you don't give yourself too much to do against the clock.
3. If the project is pretty much "full on", try to carve out some time to keep up your networking and prospecting, so that you do everything possible to reduce the chance of moving from feast to famine.

Retaining High Value Clients - Trusted Relationships

One way of looking at your business is that you are selling Trust; your prospects will buy "you" before they buy your subject matter expertise. If they like you, and believe they can trust you, then you are already moving along the pathway to assent. Trust is one of the main reasons for repeat use by a client, so what are some of the ways that you can build that level of trust?

- Trust comes from delivering results on time. If you make a promise, or commitment, and you can match it or beat it, then you are building trust. This is where the dark art of managing "scope creep" comes in!
- It also comes from delivering on or below budget. Again, they will trust what you tell them on future assignments.
- The whole way you approach prospects and clients, in particular making an effort to adapt your behaviour to match theirs, thereby creating a "meeting of minds", will also help.
- Sticking to what you are good at, and what you deserve to be paid well for, is another foundation of trust. You will gain trust and respect by being open and honest in regard to what you can and can't do.
- Keeping in touch with clients, even in between assignments, can make a contribution as well. "I saw this article and thought of you" – useful tactic to employ and generally one which is much appreciated.

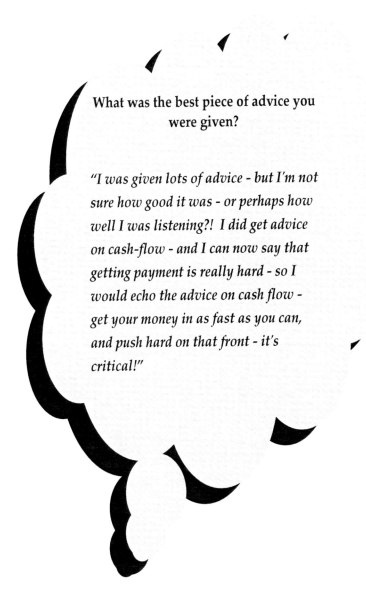

What was the best piece of advice you were given?

"I was given lots of advice - but I'm not sure how good it was - or perhaps how well I was listening?! I did get advice on cash-flow - and I can now say that getting payment is really hard - so I would echo the advice on cash flow - get your money in as fast as you can, and push hard on that front - it's critical!"

Continuously striving for a better understanding of the client's business, and his or her issues, will also bear fruit over time. In this regard, one key tip is to instil in them the confidence and belief that you do genuinely understand their business, their issues, and have them in mind when you are not in their presence.

This can set you apart from your competition and position you so that you are better placed to react to what they will need next, as opposed to merely reacting to what they need now. This will also assist you over time if, aspirationally, you would like to move from consultant to trusted advisor.

Retaining High Value Clients - Appropriate "Bag of Tools"

It is very helpful to have a "Bag of Tools" so that you have resources you can draw on as necessary, which suit the client and the situation. Someone coined the phrase "If you only have a hammer in your tool bag, you will treat every problem like a nail" ... and I have encountered people who do this and then are surprised when they get pushback from the client or prospect. The watchword is,therefore,to make sure you have a range of tools which you can apply, but don't use them at inappropriate times or in inappropriate situations.

Areas where you might want to have tools at your disposal could, by way of example, include:

- Focus Groups
- Interviewing
- Problem solving
- Innovative/creative thinking
- Relationship building
- Communication
- Strategy formulation
- Strategy implementation
- Managing strategic change
- Project Management
- Performance management and measurement
- Coaching
- Counselling
- Conflict resolution

Consultancy Framework

Key Challenges	Consultancy Models	Success Factors
• Credibility • Behaviours and Attributes • Lead Generation	• SME - Subject Matter Expert • Change Agent • Trusted Advisor	• Self-Awareness • Clarity of Purpose • Price Integrity
Routes to Market	**Sales Process**	**Tendering**
• Direct • Indirect • Other	• Qualification • Pipeline Management • Asking for the Business	• Path to Assent • Writing a Bid • Presenting a Bid
Retaining High Value Clients	**Personal Branding**	**Do's and Don'ts**
• Delivery Process • Trusted Relationship • Appropriate Bag of Tools		

There are many more that you could assemble which would fit your interests, your experience, and your proposition. The key is to put together a toolkit with which you feel comfortable and which gives you the confidence to get the job done. Be careful about including tools where your comfort level is lower. Stick with ones with which you are familiar, and/or you have been trained to use.

One tool which I use, mentioned in Chapter 2, is PRISM, which I employ to help with:

• Self-Awareness
• Team building
• Leading High Performance Teams
• Team Performance Diagnostics
• Recruitment
• 360 Reviews
• Adaptive Selling Techniques

Others which I have developed myself include the "one-page plan", which I encourage all my clients to use. It is a diagnostic tool to evaluate progress towards achieving strategic objectives (in other words, "How far have we come?").

Arm yourself with a mix of appropriate tools, either acquired externally or developed by you internally, and keep them ready for use as and when the situation calls for them. It could make a significant difference when undertaking client assignments, thereby creating happy clients!

To what extent have you had to adapt your original idea?

"I have not had to adapt my original idea yet - but business is showing signs of growing to the extent that I may have to be more selective about which clients I carry out work for - and that could cause my plans to change. Do I continue as a one man band, or work closer with others? That could be the next challenge, and one I need to start to consider."

Personal Branding - Attributes

It will be helpful to look at Attributes in the context of personal branding, particularly when it comes to business development.

We reviewed this earlier on when we looked at challenges, in that selling your services is one of the hardest things to do. Delivery is the easy bit! I think it is fair to say that selling has become a lot less confrontational and adversarial than it used to be (with notable exceptions), and a meeting of minds has become more important - remember our consideration of PRISM.

When I run my workshops, I do a little word association exercise; I say one word and ask the delegates to write down the first thing that comes into their head.

The one word is "Salesperson" - the responses I generally receive are predominantly negative, including words such as:

- Impolite
- Shallow
- Pushy
- Smoothie
- Aggressive
- Shark
- Bully
- Suit
- Sleazy
- Scumbag

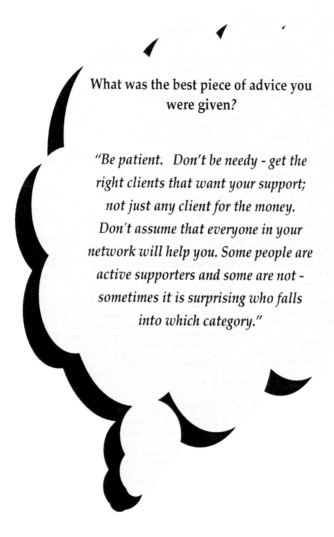

What was the best piece of advice you were given?

"Be patient. Don't be needy - get the right clients that want your support; not just any client for the money. Don't assume that everyone in your network will help you. Some people are active supporters and some are not - sometimes it is surprising who falls into which category."

It is fair to say that most of the words volunteered are not words that you would feel happy being used about yourself! Ladies and gentlemen, we therefore have a challenge.

If we are going to eat then normally we have to sell and yet we associate selling with pushy, sleazy scumbags in suits! So how do we do sales without having to risk ourselves being perceived as one or more of the negative images conjured up?

I would like to try to demystify the sales process for you and make it slightly less scary. My personal view is there are three attributes of a successful salesperson:

1. The first attribute is the ability to be liked. If you consider your own experience, you are more likely to buy from somebody you like!

2. The second attribute is the ability to listen. There is a famous saying that God gave us two ears and one mouth and we should use them in that proportion, and this is absolutely true. The good salesperson asks the right questions then shuts up and if you have asked the right questions and remain silent, the client will tell you all you need to know. Some of the best salespeople I have encountered are amongst the quietest people I know.

3. The third one is to my mind the hardest one to handle, namely the ability to enter the client's world, rather than try to drag the client into yours. That is where most people fall down. When people get into

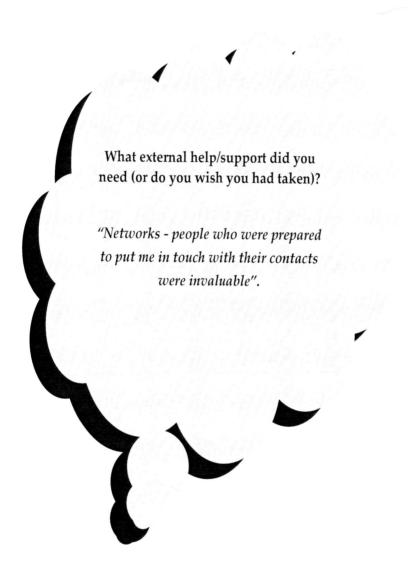

What external help/support did you
need (or do you wish you had taken)?

*"Networks - people who were prepared
to put me in touch with their contacts
were invaluable".*

the sales process and are in the thick of it, they get nervous and tense. When that happens, they revert to where they are comfortable, namely themselves and their business, and they stop talking about the client and his or her business. What you are trying to do is solve their problem in their world.

If you can master that, coupled with the other two attributes, then you have the main components of a good salesperson. You still need a process to work with and some tools at your disposal, but in terms of a sound base, you will have it.

If this topic interests you, give *Sales on a Beermat* a read - a great little book by Mike Southon and Chris West.

Personal Branding - Coherence of Image

This is a very important topic in the context of personal branding and, as I have said before, particularly with the advent of social media. Coherence of Image may not win you business but definitely reduces the likelihood of losing that business unnecessarily.

It has been on my mind quite a bit recently, in the light of some personal experiences. I am sometimes, in Winnie-the-Pooh terminology, a "bear of very little brain". Something has to happen more than once before I get the message!

Well, I saw three people in relatively quick succession at the request of people in my network, so these were all first or "exploratory" meetings. In each case, what struck me was that the person I met face-to-face was different somehow from the person I had encountered on the internet, via their website, or LinkedIn, or Twitter. And this difference was not necessarily restricted to photo versus reality, although that did apply in one of the three cases. What struck me most was that the person I met did not live up to the person I had seen on the internet; in other words, they talked a better fight in the online world than they did in the flesh.

I then started thinking about my reaction to this, and it dawned on me that I already had reservations about these people i.e. did I want to do business with them? I guess in the old world, it's a bit like falsifying or "over-egging" your CV - a dangerous game to play, as sooner or later the mask slips and you see the real person, or at least get

glimpses of them. Needless to say, my reservations were such that I have not seen any of the three a second time.

I think there are some strong ties between your personal goals, your business goals and the way you behave to achieve both. One of the factors which binds these ties together is your self-awareness, and how that translates in to a consistent manifestation of your personal brand. With that consistency come authenticity, rapport, and trust.

So, do take a little time out to check whether you really have one face to the market in what you write, what you say, and what you do.

Personal Branding - Networking

A good place to start is what Networking is not. It's not about selling; if you try to sell, you will get pushback. You can build new relationships, nurture existing ones, and promote what you do at the appropriate moment, but it's not a place to sell. It is important that you realise this in order to manage your own expectations. Remember that people buy people before they buy the underlying product or service, and so you have to cross the first hurdle before you can try to deal with the second one.

Networking is the "glue" in your marketing mix as you can see from Figure 6 on the following page. It will help you sustain interest created by your marketing collateral and activity - PR, Advertising, social media activity, talks, elevator pitches - and sustain interest and keep you in your audience's mind until they are ready either to

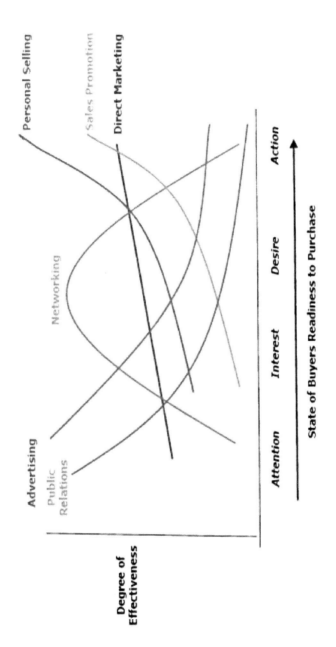

a) buy from you or b) recommend you to someone else who needs what you can offer. Then and only then can you start the sales process which we have talked about earlier.

For a typical consultant, around 70% of your business development time will be spent making contacts, establishing rapport, and building empathy and trust. Only 20% will be proposal-related, and 10% negotiating and closing. So the networking piece is an important component. In support of that, my top five tips for successful networking are as follows:

1. Try several events until you find the one that works best for you, and go several times; there are no short cuts and you need to get known, which takes time.
2. Do not just latch on to the one person in the room whom you recognise; make some new contacts.
3. Let them talk about their business first; you will get your chance.
4. Think about how you can help them, even if there is no immediate business in it for you.
5. If you promise to do something, do make sure you follow-up.

Oh, and don't forget to smile and look like you are enjoying it!

Consultancy Framework

Key Challenges	Consultancy Models	Success Factors
• Credibility • Behaviours and Attributes • Lead Generation	• SME - Subject Matter Expert • Change Agent • Trusted Advisor	• Self-Awareness • Clarity of Purpose • Price Integrity
Routes to Market	**Sales Process**	**Tendering**
• Direct • Indirect • Other	• Qualification • Pipeline Management • Asking for the Business	• Path to Assent • Writing a Bid • Presenting a Bid
Retaining High Value Clients	**Personal Branding**	**Do's and Don'ts**
• Delivery Process • Trusted Relationship • Appropriate Bag of Tools	• Attributes • Coherence of Image • Networking	

Do's and Don'ts - 10 Habits of Top Consultants

I sense it is time for a small aspirational piece. With that in mind, I have highlighted 10 Habits of Successful Consultants – always good to have something to aim at!

1. They ensure the quality of their work. It's really easy to let standards slip as you get busy, but good consultants are obsessive about maintaining standards, so that technical excellence is taken as a given.
2. They have a sixth sense that tells them when there is a vacuum which may prevent successful completion of a project, and they will assume ownership and provide leadership if that is what they consider necessary to keep things on track.
3. They are very delivery oriented, so they will be focused on outcomes, and be driven to ensure that the project completes on time and to specification.
4. From an emotional intelligence standpoint, they have a high degree of self-awareness, which they constantly develop and employ in their communication and relationship-building with others.
5. They use their self-awareness to learn how to adapt their behaviour in order to better match the behaviour preferences of people they are required to work with.
6. They tend to be punctual.
7. They prepare thoroughly for all meetings and events.
8. They work hard on their listening skills.
9. They anticipate potential alternative outcomes and developments, so that they can react accordingly, and are better equipped to cope with the unexpected and take challenges in their stride.

10. They tend to have a "Plan B" up their sleeve for use in case of need.

How do you stack up against this list? I recommend that you reflect on it, and then plan out some personal development time if need be.

Do's and Don'ts - 10 Disastrous Strategies

We will consider the potential "own goal" areas of consultancy. These are not included on the grounds that they are theoretically possible; I have seen all of them occur (not all as a result of my efforts, I would add!).

1. Making promises and failing to deliver. This can happen for a variety of reasons - saying you can do something when you can't, getting absorbed by something more interesting, double-booking yourself, or simply losing track of what you have promised and to whom. This is where it really pays to have a good sales pipeline system, and a good PA!

2. Getting out of your depth. This is really building on the first point above. Do not take on something which takes you away from your core competence and area of subject matter expertise, or something where the size and scale is such that it's too big for you to handle.

3. Wasting the client's time. This can be anything from engaging in small talk when the client wants to get down to business, through to calling unnecessary meetings which are not going to take the work forward. Don't forget to adapt your style of working to match the client's style better.

4. Creating change for its own sake. "If it isn't broke, don't fix it," still holds good today. Clients will actually respect you more if you advise them that certain aspects of their operation remain fit for purpose.

5. Confusing symptoms with disease and curing the wrong problem. Do keep an open mind when taking on a new challenge that the perceived problem is

Our survey showed

that the biggest

learning point was

picking up "best

practice" from others

indeed the real problem. Sometimes it isn't! I was once asked by the board of a small business to work with the second tier of management as they were holding back the company's growth. When I worked with them, I discovered the tricky reality that the business was in fact being held back by the board, not the second tier!

6. Trying to impose your own values. You have to respect a company's culture, and you must remain sensitive to it at all times.

7. Creating an inappropriate attachment to a client. This is as dangerous in consultancy as it is in any other business context.

8. Failing to be candid. It takes courage sometimes to tell a client what they need to hear, as opposed to what they want to hear, but you owe it to yourself to be honest and to maintain your integrity.

9. Have a "one-size-fits-all" approach. We have already considered the fact that "if the only tool you have is a hammer, you will treat every problem as a nail". Beware applying the wrong solution to the wrong problem.

10. Lose professional detachment and focus. Sometimes it helps to have veins of ice! However hard it may be at times, you need to maintain an aura of calm and stay in control. If a situation becomes and looks set to remain untenable, then plan your exit in a dignified, sensitive and timely manner.

I am sure we have all slipped up somewhere in terms of this list, but the more we can guard against it, the greater the likelihood that we can create value as opposed to destroy it, and enhance our reputation in the process.

Our survey showed the top three tips are:

1. Network, Network, Network

2. Prepare for things to take longer than expected

3. Be absolutely clear about positioning

Do's and Don'ts - 10 Time Management Tips

One of the challenges with being your own boss is that there is no-one else to tell you what to do and by when. It is therefore worthwhile considering how you manage your time. This is my Achilles heel by the way! I've had to work very hard at this and will occasionally "backslide", so I need to be vigilant. This is where having a good mentor and a good PA come in, as they will both "nag" you in different ways if this is an issue (in my case, in a nice but forceful way) and make you focus on what is important.

In this section then, we will consider some top tips on time management. I try to practise these, and sometimes I succeed!

1. Enjoy the freedom of running your own life. Obviously, you have to be mindful of client expectations, but if it suits you and the family to take time off during the week and work part of the weekend, you can do it.
2. Use lists to create forward momentum - for the month, week, and day - and tick things off as you do them.
3. Don't waste time on issues that could be easily delegated or that you are not suited to doing.
4. Don't procrastinate over non-essential decisions.
5. Do what feels right at the time. Whilst you can't put things off forever, there may be some that you need to be in the mood for if you are going to be at your most effective.
6. Maintain a sanctum sanctorum - part of your home which is either clearly earmarked as your office or you treat as your office, so you (and everyone else) knows you are in work mode.

7. Do not be afraid to spend money to maximise efficiency, either via people or systems, or a combination of both.
8. Be selfish with your time. I will give anyone an hour of my time for free, but after that, the meter is running. It will discourage the time-wasters - and they are out there!
9. Plan your long-term time investment. If you know you have a major piece of work to deliver in three months' time, don't leave the planning and preparation to week four of month three!
10. Allow for the unexpected. Try to keep some slack time that you can use for urgent meetings, unanticipated client requests, and the vagaries of the transport system.

A good place to start is with what one of my clients christened a "dead-time audit". It's very simple; set up an excel spreadsheet for seven days, and break it in to 15 minute components. Colour various activities (billable work, marketing, networking, admin, travel etc.) and complete the spreadsheet. It will give you a very simple graphic of how you are spending your time, and how you can prioritise improvements. I would guarantee you at least one surprise.

Consultancy Framework

Key Challenges	Consultancy Models	Success Factors
• *Credibility* • *Behaviours and Attributes* • *Lead Generation*	• *SME - Subject Matter Expert* • *Change Agent* • *Trusted Advisor*	• *Self-Awareness* • *Clarity of Purpose* • *Price Integrity*
Routes to Market	**Sales Process**	**Tendering**
• *Direct* • *Indirect* • *Other*	• *Qualification* • *Pipeline Management* • *Asking for the Business*	• *Path to Assent* • *Writing a Bid* • *Presenting a Bid*
Retaining High Value Clients	**Personal Branding**	**Do's and Don'ts**
• *Delivery Process* • *Trusted Relationship* • *Appropriate Bag of Tools*	• *Attributes* • *Coherence of Image* • *Networking*	• *10 Habits of Top Consultants* • *10 Disastrous Strategies* • *10 Time Management Tips*

Consultancy Health Check - Self-Diagnostic (Figure 7)

Score yourself out of 10 on each of the 10 issues (0 being not very good, and 10 being outstanding)

	ISSUE	Score
1	I have a strategic plan for where I want to take my business in the medium-term	
2	I have a business plan for the current year to use as my operational map and route, with associated goals and objectives	
3	I will be working to a robust financial plan based on researched assumptions	
4	I will be working to a sales process which helps me to win the business I want and avoid potential timewasters and bad debts	
5	I will be working to a delivery process which helps me to create satisfied clients who buy more and/or refer others	
6	I have worked out the optimum marketing mix for my business, including routes to market and social media strategy	
7	I have established the network I need to enable my business to flourish	
8	I know what makes me distinctive and can articulate it	
9	I have worked out my personal branding	
10	I have quality and comprehensive support around me	
TOTAL		

If your score is <30 *You should probably talk your idea through with someone and decide what you should do next*
If your score is <60 *You are probably not ready to launch yet - more preparatory work to do*
If your score is >60 *You can press on with some confidence, but keep looking for improvements*

Epilogue...

We are approaching the end of our journey together. A few closing thoughts and comments for you.

Please find on the previous page a short self-diagnostic for you (Figure 7). It will help you to decide whether you are "good to go" or not.

You may recall that I suggested earlier that you should create a one-page plan. Well I have created three additional templates for you to help you with your financial planning and modelling.

In Appendix 1, you will find:

- a simple profit and loss forecast
- an associated cash flow forecast
- a "flash" report to give you an example of how to monitor your progress.

We haven't talked much about infrastructure, apart from my encouraging you to surround yourself with quality. There are five basic legs to your supporting infrastructure, and they are:

1. Legal
2. Accounting
3. People
4. IT
5. Insurance

Value Chain Model
Figure 8

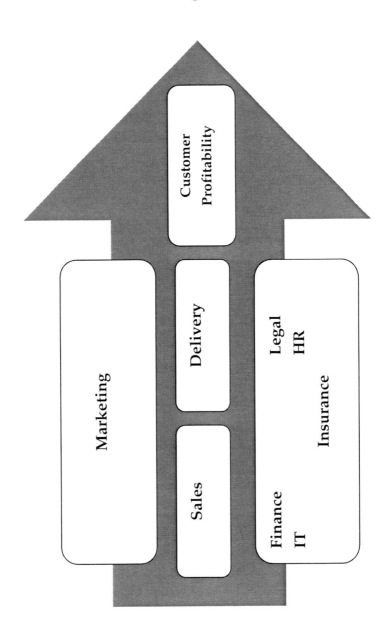

Customer Profitability

Marketing

Delivery

Sales

Legal

HR

Insurance

Finance

IT

I am indebted to five of my closest associates who have each prepared a "top tips" list for you, which you will find in Appendix 2.

We have considered social media, and in Appendix 3 you will find some insights from my son James on this topic. I hope you have found this book helpful. I want to leave you with a final diagram (Figure 8, opposite) to help you remember the salient points:

- Marketing is not a one-off exercise; it goes on forever. Make sure people understand what makes you different, and make sure you live up to it. If your market moves, make sure you move with it.
- It's all about clients (Sales) and satisfying them (Delivery) so that they come back for more and/or recommend others.
- Don't forget to invest in the Infrastructure (Finance, Legal, IT, HR, Insurance) to make your business a well-oiled machine.
- And finally, do not lose sight of what makes you and your business special; that should be represented in the profitability to you of your customers and therefore your profit margin.

I wish you every success!

Appendix 1

Financial Planning and Modelling

Appendix 1

The Profit and Loss Forecast and the Cash Flow Forecast are based on the one-page plan. But they only become worthwhile documents if you can find a way of using the assumptions in them to check how you are doing as the year unfolds.

So we could use a "Flash Report", in this case showing your sixth month of trading, and based on the associated Profit and Loss Forecast and Cash Flow Forecasts.

Let's imagine for a moment we do a check at six months with some illustrative numbers. If you remember we wanted to be on a run rate by this stage of six billable days a month at £1,000 per day. We are indeed getting £1,000 per day but we are doing eight days. So we are ahead overall of our first two KPIs. Further good news, we have kept our costs to less than 20% of turnover.

And finally our liquidity ratio is very healthy. Remember, what this means is that you look at what you have in the bank, add to that what you are owed, take off what you owe and hope that the ratio is better than 1:1 i.e. if the business stopped on that day you would be in a good position to pay all your liabilities as they fell due. If it was the other way round, you would only be surviving with the goodwill of the bank and your creditors.

The non-financial KPIs, around social media activity, are a bit of a mixed bag, and are worthy of further investigation , but more to understand their implications better than because of some form of crisis.

We have checked, and you are not in a coma, so we can press ahead. If the KPIs and the Flash Report had shown something worrying, we could have taken immediate action.

Cash Flow Forecast

	JAN	FEB	MAR	APR	MAY	JUN	JUL	AUG	SEP	OCT	NOV	DEC
Cash b/f	1,000	1,000	1,600	2,200	2,800	4,000	5,200	6,400	8,200	10,000	11,800	14,200
Sales	0	3,000	3,000	3,000	6,000	6,000	6,000	9,000	9,000	9,000	12,000	12,000
Total Cash	1,000	4,000	4,600	5,200	8,800	10,000	11,200	15,400	17,200	19,000	23,800	26,200
Overhead	0	600	600	600	1200	1200	1200	1800	1800	1800	2400	2400
Net Cash	1,000	3,400	4,000	4,600	7,600	8,800	10,000	13,600	15,400	17,200	21,400	23,800
Dividend/Salary	0	1,800	1,800	1,800	3,600	3,600	3,600	5,400	5,400	5,400	7,200	7,200
Cash c/f	1,000	1,600	2,200	2,800	4,000	5,200	6,400	8,200	10,000	11,800	14,200	16,600

Assumptions
- £1000 put in as opening capital
- Dividend/Salary paid 1 month in arrears
- All debtors pay 1 month in arrears
- All creditors paid one month in arrears
- As per the one-page plan
- Reserve (25%) established to ensure business stays cash positive and tax liabilities can be met as they fall due.
- VAT ignored
- No allowance for set-up (as opposed to maintenance) costs e.g. pc,laptop,printer,website
- All costs re Marketing and Sales and Infrastructure included as overhead

Profit and Loss Forecast

	JAN	FEB	MAR	APR	MAY	JUN	JUL	AUG	SEP	OCT	NOV	DEC	TOT
Sales	3,000	3,000	3,000	6,000	6,000	6,000	9,000	9,000	9,000	12,000	12,000	12,000	**90,000**
Cost of Sales	0	0	0	0	0	0	0	0	0	0	0	0	**0**
Gross Profit	3,000	3,000	3,000	6,000	6,000	6,000	9,000	9,000	9,000	12,000	12,000	12,000	**90,000**
Overhead	600	600	600	1200	1200	1200	1800	1800	1800	2400	2400	2400	**18,000**
Net Profit	2,400	2,400	2,400	4,800	4,800	4,800	7,200	7,200	7,200	9,600	9,600	9,600	**72,000**
Reserve	600	600	600	1200	1200	1200	1800	1800	1800	2400	2400	2400	**18,000**
Dividend/Salary	1,800	1,800	1,800	3,600	3,600	3,600	5,400	5,400	5,400	7,200	7,200	7,200	**54,000**

Assumptions

- As per the one-page plan
- Reserve (25%) established to ensure business stays cash positive and tax liabilities can be met as they fall due.
- VAT ignored
- No allowance for set-up (as opposed to maintenance) costs e.g. pc,laptop,printer,website
- All costs re Marketing and Sales and Infrastructure included as overhead
- All work undertakne by self as opposed to associates

Flash Report
Consultancy Name
Monthly Financial Reporting
Month: 6

	Flash Report	Budget
Financial results		
Sales	£8,000	£6,000
Cost of Sales	£0	£0
Gross Profit	£8,000	£6,000
Overhead	£1,200	£1,200
Net Profit	£6,800	£4,800
Reserve	£1,700	£1,200
Dividend	£5,100	£3,600
KPI's		
Billable Day Rate	£1,000	£1,000
Revenue Run Rate	8 days	6 days
Costs	£1,200	£1,200
Liquidity Ratio	8:1	1:5:1
Increase in Website hits	8%	10%
Increase in LinkedIn hits	11%	10%
Increase in Twitter followers	7%	10%
Increase in Newsletter subscribers	4%	10%

Appendix 2

Top Tips

Top Tips for Start-ups
Legal - The Legal Director

The Legal Director
Legal advice from a business perspective

1.   Business format

Do you want to incorporate and set up a limited company? Or for now, is it just you and a website? Most businesses choose to set up a company as this gives them the protection of limited legal liability in case it all goes wrong, and will lend an air of credibility to your business. New companies can be set up quickly and cheaply through Companies House's easy-to-use online incorporation tool.

2.   Business name

Is anyone else already trading with a similar name? Check the business name you want to use is available as a website domain and (if you are going to incorporate a company or LLP) at Companies House. Even if the exact one you want is available, avoid names that could be confused with an existing business.

3.   Shareholders/Partnership Agreement

If you are going into business with a partner, or your friends and family are putting money into your venture, then you should have an agreement covering things like the management and control of the business, and the issue and transfer of shares. Think of it as a "pre-nup": what do you expect from your partners, how are you going to run the business on a day-to-day basis, and what will you do if you fall out?

4.   Terms and Conditions

Before you start trading, you will need to think about writing some T&Cs for dealing with your customers. Make sure you understand what your obligations are in terms of the quality of your products or standard of service, delivery, and refunds. Always insist on trading with your customers on your own T&Cs. If you are selling goods to the public then you need to be aware of things like the Distance Selling Regulations that specify what information you must give to customers, and an unconditional right to cancel and get a full refund in the first seven days. If you are accepting payment by credit card or offering other credit terms, you may need a Consumer Credit License.

5.   Employees

At first it might just be you and your business partner, but if everything goes according to plan, you may soon need to hire people. You will need to give them an employment contract if they are employees, or agree terms of engagement with them if they are freelancers. If you are hiring foreign nationals, you will need make sure they are eligible to work in the UK. You should also understand the rights your employees will have.

6.   Intellectual property

Keep your know-how and proprietary data safe and use a confidentiality agreement if you are going to disclose it. Applying for patents and trademarks is expensive and can take a long time, and is only effective if you are prepared to enforce (very expensive and time-consuming). You can use the ™ symbol without registering a trademark. Copyright arises automatically on the creation of an original work, including software, so make sure you have an audit trail so you can prove that you created / wrote / designed the work.

7.   Business Plan

Does your business plan contain confidential or proprietary information about your products or services? Include an appropriate disclaimer and confidentiality statement on the first page, and in the footer "© [Name] Ltd, 2013. Confidential" before you distribute it to third parties. Consider whether you should ask recipients to sign a specific confidentiality agreement.

8.   Data Protection

If you are collecting personal data, then make sure you register with the Information Commissioner (quick and inexpensive) and that you understand the rules on handling data.

9.   Raising Money

If you are looking to raise money from investors, you need to make sure you don't fall foul of the rules on financial promotions - what you can say and to whom. If you get it wrong, your investors can ask for their money back so this is one area where you must obtain specialist advice.

10.   Dealing with Lawyers

It is likely you will need to use a lawyer at some point in your start-up phase. Make sure you understand what you are asking your lawyer to do, and what you will and won't pay for, and push for a fixed fee. Don't be afraid to say if you think you're not getting value for money. The best business lawyers can be a real asset to your growing business and become a trusted advisor. Ask for a package deal that includes support on ad hoc queries over the first few months of trading (note that you may be able to access this kind of legal support service through membership of organisations like the IoD or your local Chamber of Commerce).

Top Tips for Start-ups Accounting

1. Tax Structure: Sole Trader vs. Limited Company vs. Partnership

If you are starting a business, it is important to ensure that you choose the right tax structure. There are advantages and disadvantages to each of the different tax structures, and it is therefore important that you obtain advice from an accountant as to the most suitable structure for your current circumstances, business plan and future goals.

2. Registering for VAT

If you're a business and the goods or services you provide count as what's known as 'taxable supplies', you'll have to register for VAT if either your turnover for the previous 12 months has gone over a specific limit, called the 'VAT threshold' (at time of print: £77,000), or if you think your turnover will soon reach this limit. However, you can voluntarily register for VAT if you would like to. There are different VAT schemes, annual VAT (which means you only need to submit a VAT return once a year), normal VAT on an accrual basis (returns are submitted quarterly, based on invoice date), normal VAT on a cash basis (returns will be submitted quarterly, based on when you have received/paid the money), the Flat Rate VAT scheme (a set percentage of your gross turnover depending on your industry is payable, ranging between 8 – 14%). It is important to ensure you register for the best VAT scheme suitable to your circumstance, so ensure to obtain advice regarding this from your accountant.

3. Filing Responsibilities of a Limited Company

If you set-up a limited company, you will be responsible to submit a set of abbreviated financial accounts to Companies House nine months after your accounting period end date and a full set of financial accounts together with your corporation tax return to HMRC 12 months after your accounting period end date. You are also required to complete an annual return to Companies House (annual shuttle return) each year. This can be completed online or via a paper return, and is normally due 12 months after incorporation. Please also see filing obligations relating to VAT and PAYE under the relevant sections.

4. Personal Tax Returns & Deadlines

If you are self-employed, a director of a limited company, you have rental income, owe HMRC tax on any other source of income, or if HMRC sends you a tax return to complete, then you are required to complete a personal tax return for the financial year (6th April – 5th April). Your tax return will be due for submission by 31st October if you are filing a paper return, or by 31st January of the following year if you are submitting it online. Your tax payment for the year will be payable by 31st January, together with a 50% payment on account towards your next year's tax liability with the other 50% payable on 31st July of the following year.

5.   Claimable Expenses

All expenses incurred wholly, exclusively and necessarily for business purposes, can be claimed through the company or deducted from your self-employed income. Please ensure to keep all receipts/invoices for any expenses incurred. Please note that certain expenses can be paid through the business, but are not tax deductible, i.e. entertainment, and will therefore be added back when calculating Corporation Tax or Income Tax.

6.   Employing Staff

If you are considering employing staff, you will be required to set up and administer a PAYE scheme with HMRC, which you can outsource. You will have to calculate PAYE/NI on all payments that an employee receives, and you will need to make these payments to HMRC by the 19th of the following month. You will also be required to provide all employees employed at 5th April with a P60 by 31st May following the end of the tax year or a P45 when an employee leaves your employment. You will also be required to file monthly payroll returns to HMRC declaring the salaries and taxes due for the month before the employees are paid.

7.   Credit Control

In any successful business, CASH IS KING, and therefore it is imperative that credit control is exercised frequently. Work together with your accounting function (in-house or outsourced) to set these controls and procedures in place and prepare a monthly cash flow statement to ensure you will be able to meet your short-term and long-term liabilities.

8.   Paperwork & Filing

You are required to keep a paper trail of all invoices, expenses, bank statements, credit cards etc. for a minimum of six years. Ensure that your filing is kept up to date. We recommend filing all invoices in sequential order and all supplier invoices per supplier in date order which will make it easier to obtain paperwork in future. It is also advisable to write on the paperwork to which account it has been posted to and the date it was entered and paid.

9.   Accounting Packages

It is advisable to enter your accounting records and transactions into an accounting package from day one, as it will assist you in obtaining useful management information efficiently and effectively and it will reduce your accountant's fee for preparing your statutory accounts at year end. QuickBooks, SAGE and Xero are widely used amongst small to medium-sized companies; however it is advised to obtain advice from an accountant as to the most beneficial accounting package to suit your particular circumstances, type of business and your long-term goals.

10. Accounting Function: In-house or Outsourced

There are advantages and disadvantages of both, however outsourcing the accounting function for small to medium-sized businesses can be very beneficial, providing the following benefits amongst others: expert services at a fraction of the price, no recruitment/management fees, no office expenses, continuity is provided with no need for re-hiring or re-training, and many more. It is important to review both options and choose the most optimum solution for your business.

Top Tips for Start-ups People

peoplerisksolutions

1. Recruitment

You are bound to need people working with you in your new business. Recruiting the right individuals is important. A good place to start is using your network to identify known candidates. You could also place adverts online; there are several cost-effective job boards which can harvest lots of CVs. Bear in mind that if you get someone with 75% of the skills you need, you are doing well. If you still don't find someone, then use a recruitment agency, but make sure that you negotiate a good fee rate upfront. Always carry out thorough interviews and ensure that you draw up a list of competencies and skills that you want for the job.

2. Reference checks

Once you have identified the right person, make sure you carry out independent reference checks before they join. Many people are not completely honest on their CVs. Do not accept previously written "To whom they may concern" references. Always contact previous employers. You may wish to conduct a criminal records bureau (CRB) check as well; this website may be helpful www.crb.gov.uk. There are also agencies who offer a full reference service such as www.kroll.com.

3.   Pay

An important part of the business dynamic is how much to pay yourself and your team. Take advice from your accountants regarding tax because this will drive the pay structure. Make sure that you appoint someone competent to run your payroll and to manage issues like PAYE, P60s and P45s and the new legislation about live pay data for HMRC. Pay is likely to be one of your largest overheads and so make sure that you do not overpay staff. Try and be creative such as offering commission for increased sales so that your increased income can improve pay for some staff. Finally, do not forget about pensions; recent legislation means that even small companies need to make pension provisions for staff.

4.   Employment contracts

If you employ staff, make sure that you give them some form of employment contract. This should lay out key aspects of employment such as salary, notice period, holidays, benefits, disciplinary and grievance procedures. There are several HR outsource businesses that can provide low-cost help such as Right Hand HR - www.rhhr.com. The main aim of the contract is to avoid any misunderstandings later on.

5.   Organisational Structure

Most small firms have a fairly flat reporting structure. However, as you employ more people, it is important to be clear about who does what and who is responsible for what. A brief job description for each job including who the individual reports to will avoid problems later on. This will also help when you appraise performance.

6. Policies and procedures

It will be useful to have some basic people policies and procedures once you employ more than two or three staff. The main reason is to try and capture all the small employment issues before they arise. A staff handbook can outline how you will deal with issues such as maternity leave, disciplinary issues, compassionate leave, benefits and any restrictions post-employment. As the business grows, you can add policies as appropriate.

7. Performance management

Most people want to know how they are performing at work. You should have some form of performance appraisal process. As a minimum, formally appraise everyone at least once a year. Use company and individual objectives to ensure that everyone's efforts are focused in the same direction. Also take into account learning and development for your team. Improving skills will end up adding value to the business overall.

8. Dealing with disputes

When you employ people, there will inevitably be disputes. Make sure that you always treat everyone fairly and be consistent when dealing with problems. Make sure that you follow due process if you have to discipline anyone - failure to do so can be regarded as unfair and claims can be made accordingly via an employment tribunal. The ACAS website is helpful in this regard - www.acas.org.uk.

9.   Non-Executive Directors

As the business grows, it is worthwhile appointing non-executive directors. These are typically people who have expertise in areas that you do not have already and can advise you on how to take the business forward. They may be Marketing, Finance, HR or IT specialists. Initially, they may be unpaid but in due course, you should pay them a nominal fee.

10.   Succession planning

In order to ensure business growth, you should plan for changes of personnel. People leave firms for a range of unexpected reasons so it is worth thinking about who could replace key roles. Some entrepreneurs are always interviewing potential candidates in order to keep the people pipeline alive. It is also important to provide development opportunities where possible. Bear in mind that the people who help you start up the business may not be the right people to take the business forward in the future.

Tops Tips for Start-ups
Information Technology

1.   IT Budget

Budgeting and choosing the right equipment for the tasks that are required at the beginning, and that will be useful in the future for your business, is fundamental. Many small businesses do not realise the competitive advantages offered by technology, as they don't have the resources or expertise to evaluate or implement the solutions available to them. Another key problem is that many people try to spend as little as possible on technology and therefore disregard the potential cost savings that can be generated if they get it right.

Investment into IT systems is important, and below are some key points relating to investment.

2.   Creating an Internet Identity

Domain name and email addresses should be the first thing you think about. Choose an unused domain name and register it with a professional organisation who can offer multiple email accounts and web/storage space. Choose a domain name relevant to the name of the company or a name which directly relates to the company's type of business; this will help later to self-promote your website on search engines.

From the chosen office location, organise an internet connection. Research the suppliers available to you at that location e.g. BT, O2 or Virgin. There are deals and discounts available when you combine internet and telephone services through the same supplier.

3.   Protecting your identity

If your business uses email, you'll be targeted at some stage. The main problem is that such attacks are becoming more sophisticated. The malicious software used develops in your system and the threat of someone accessing valuable company information becomes more likely.

Fraudulent emails are increasingly authentic in appearance, purporting to originate from various sources, from banks to potential clients. The process is known as "phishing", and such emails will contain a link to a website on which you will be asked to re-confirm some details or confirm a password with the aim of stealing your details and using them to access your account. Files coming into an organisation downloaded from the internet and transported on a flash drive or disc, for example, can also be dangerous. These can contain malicious software, generally known as malware, that is sophisticated enough to hide itself from anti-virus software. Malware can log any key strokes that you make on the keyboard and send the information elsewhere when you connect to the web. This means that passwords and bank account details could be at risk, along with private company documents and emails.

It is recommended that you have a company policy to deal with such issues. Education and awareness for staff about the dangers out there is all important and for most organisations it is the first line of defence. It is as much the responsibility of the individual employee as it is for management to be aware of identity fraud and protect their own and the company's interests. This could mean regulating the use of external hard drives, including iPods, flash keys and discs with dubious or uncertain origins in the workplace and, moreover, informing staff of the ways in which criminals might try to access their private information.

Data leakage is also an increasing problem. For businesses, corporate identity is as precious as their staff and preventing information from getting out could be down to something as simple as warning people not to share too much on social networking websites or not to send too much valuable company information across the internet.

4.   Router and Firewall

Purchase a good brand wireless router. This may come free with the internet connection. Ensure that it has a built-in firewall, as this will help to secure any equipment that will be connected to the internet. The router creates the connection automatically between your network and the internet via your ISP - Internet Service Provider. A router, rather than just a modem, is used because it uses NAT, Network Address Translation, as part of its Firewall. This works by converting (translating) the internet address, TCPIP protocol, to a private address range on the inside of your network.

Anyone trying to attack the external address will not be able to penetrate the firewall unless there are ports open to let traffic through.

5.   Network

For a small network, the router that the ISP supplies will probably suffice, as it will usually come with four Ethernet Ports (normally 100MB).

In addition, the router will normally be wireless enabled, which can be connected to a plethora of different devices - PCs, laptops, wireless printers, PDAs, phones and games consoles.

If you require more than four hard-wired devices, then a small Gigabyte network switch would be ideal, with 5 to 48 ports on a single switch, desk to switches 5 to 16 ports and rack mountable switches available from 16 to 48 ports. These switches are available in many price ranges and complex abilities. For larger organisations, they may use PoE, Power over Ethernet switches, which can power IP telephones, wireless access points, cameras and many other PoE enabled devices.

6.   Server

For small and large networks, it is important to have a server to centrally store the company's data. For fast response and resilient availability, choose and design your server to cope with the company's immediate needs. In the future, storage can always be added on, should it be required.

If the server is to run databases such as SQL or similar, make sure that the processor is well above the stated minimum specification for the application. Memory for servers is more expensive than for standard PCs but it is very important to have enough for the server to comfortably run all of the systems it has to. If a server runs light on memory, it will slow down and use the hard discs to swap information that it is required and this will make the server slow to respond and will shorten the life of the hard drives.

7. Software

When installing software onto a computer system, you can never be too careful, especially if you keep important customer information stored there. Even if the software has come from a trusted source, complications can arise so it would be wise to take precautions beforehand. It's always best, therefore, to make a back-up copy of important information before installing any new software.

You should try to scan all floppy discs, CD-ROMs, and DVD-ROMs with your anti-virus software before copying files from them or installing software that they contain. You never know if a nasty virus is lurking on a seemingly innocent disc.

Never install pirated software onto your computer. Illegal copies of software, such as those downloaded from hacker websites or sourced from file-sharing programs, may contain hidden viruses.

Before installing any software, be sure you know exactly what is being copied onto your system. Sometimes apparently innocuous software can contain viruses or Trojans that might take control of your computer. This is a particular danger with file-sharing programs that allow you to trade music or videos.

8.   Anti-virus

Anti-virus protection also plays an important role as it should safeguard you from the harmful viruses, spyware and those annoying spammed messages on your email. There are many free and paid-for anti-virus products available on the market but it is important to make sure that the one you chose is adequate for your needs and that you have it running up-to-date on all of your computers.

You should regularly check and scan your computers for viruses and spyware, as many infections are designed to steal your identity and passwords and can appear like Trojans at any time.

In addition, you should be careful when registering to anything online that it is provided by reputable company and that you are on a secure website. This is always indicated by the address starting with https:// or a locked padlock somewhere on your browser application. It is sometimes a good idea to use a temporary or online mail account when subscribing to an unknown source, so that your normal mail data is protected should the new source turn out to be bogus.

9.   UPS

Protecting your hardware from power spikes and disturbances is important. Laptops are usually alright as they predominately run on their own internal battery. PCs, servers, routers and other network components will require mains filtering and battery backup, as data corruption or loss can occur if the power is lost or spiked to your equipment. UPS (Uninterruptable Power Suppliers) are available in all sizes and affordability but don't scrimp on these. Ideally, you would want it to stay running for at least 10 minutes, in order to give you a chance to save that important document that you have spent hours working on. Basic multi-port units are available, which can maintain power for a few devices that would possibly lose data if the power was to fail. Recommended devices to be protected would be PCs and servers; other devices such as printers, network switches and routers do not require UPS protection but will require surge protection to protect them from spikes and mains interference.

10.   Backup

A small network should have at least one form of data backup e.g. tape, CD/DVD, external hard disc or off-site backup. It is not ideal to keep all your data in one place where it can be vulnerable to fire, theft or data corruption. It is always recommended that you keep a copy of your data in a physically different location to the workplace, so that should the original data be lost, it can be replaced easily.

There are now many organisations and ISPs who can supply you with off-site or internet-based backups and most of these work very well, utilising your internet bandwidth at night when your requirement to use this is less. Always make sure that with whatever backup you choose that you regularly check the logs and periodically perform data restores from whatever source you have chosen, in order to verify that the backup is working and so that you understand how to do this in the event of actually needing the data back.

There are ten common mistakes made with technology in the workplace:

1. Assuming that IT can be easily deployed and managed without expert support
2. Failing to test equipment thoroughly with real-life scenarios
3. Poor testing of security vulnerabilities
4. Not setting out service requirements with IT providers at the outset
5. Ineffectively aligning IT to business needs
6. Focusing on short-term cost gains due to time pressures and not the longer-term productivity and revenue generating benefits of IT
7. Choosing IT that cannot cope with rapid changes in business needs
8. Not planning ahead so you can scale up your technology needs appropriately
9. Having the wrong return on investment expectations of technology which impacts badly on the bottom line
10. Cutting IT budget or thinking managing IT in-house will be easier and more cost-effective in hard times.

Choosing the right hardware and software is key to success when integrating IT into your new business.

Top Tips for Start-ups
Insurance

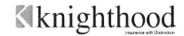

Insurance is an essential part of any business' considerations, especially for start-up companies when it is important to ensure your cover is as wide as possible to give you the correct protection, but also to ensure costs are competitive.

The ABI (Association of British Insurers) recently released statistics showing that only 23% of companies that suffer a major loss are still trading two years later. This could be because they were foolish enough to start trading without insurance but the most likely explanation is that the insurance did not respond adequately following the loss. This could be because the cover was inadequate or because the policyholder did not understand what was required of them in respect of the policy's terms, conditions and warranties.

To consider this in context, it is important to understand the whole basis of insurance. It is, in simple terms, "risk transfer". You are asking somebody else to bear the burden of some of the risks - mainly financial - that you would be unable to carry by yourself. For example, few businesses would be able to, say, replace their building or all of their stock if either were to be destroyed in a fire, storm or flood. Similarly, it has to be recognised that as a society, we are becoming more litigious and you should protect yourself against any potential liability you may incur for injury, property damage or financial loss.

The ABI also recently reported that of every pound paid out in claims by insurers, 83% related to legal costs, substantially inflating the costs of even a minor claim.

So where do you go for the best advice on the financial exposures you face and the insurance you need? Some insurance companies are set up to deal on a direct basis but can only offer you their own products and are unable to advise you on products not within their policy range. In our opinion, the best course of action is to talk with an insurance broker who will be able to offer you access to a wide range of insurers and specialist schemes, to ensure you get the widest cover at a competitive price. But not all brokers are the same, and below are a number of handy tips you should consider in your selection process:

1.   Selecting a recommended broker

Ask industry peers, friends and even family if they are able to positively recommend an insurance broker. Speak to two or three different firms for advice and then compare who is most responsive to your needs and instils you with confidence. Give weight to the broker that will offer to meet with you to discuss your business and help identify the risks you face and try to agree some service standard levels that meet your particular requirements. Ensure that they fully understand your business and ask them who will be providing ongoing support and avoid telesales companies to whom you will just be a name on a screen.

Often the only time you find the true value of your insurance is in the event of a claim so ask the broker how they help you with claims and avoid any who passes you on directly to the insurers.

It is possible to buy online but there can be pitfalls. Informed product face-to-face advice is very often the better option.

2.   Make sure you get written quotations

Make sure you are supplied with full details of all terms and conditions that will apply, before giving instructions to go on cover. Read all documents carefully and ensure that you are able to comply in full. If you cannot, you should let your broker know.

3.   Work with the broker to carefully assess your own risk

There is no benefit to over-insuring, and to under-insure could leave you in serious financial difficulties, so make sure all of your sums insured are carefully calculated.

Similarly, make sure you have accurate estimates of your turnover and projected wages and estimated gross profits, etc.

4.   Professional Risks

In addition to obvious business exposures such as asset protection, etc., it is important that you consider professional risks which could, amongst other things, include financial covers such as Directors & Offices Liability insurance, Libel and Slander insurance, Fidelity insurance, Trustees Indemnity insurance and the like.

5.   Make sure you meet your legal requirements

You are required by law to have Employers' Liability insurance. This is required by statute and you will face penalties if you do not have the correct insurance.

Similarly, if you operate cars, vans, lorries or other motorised equipment on a public highway, you are required to arrange at least Third Party insurance under the requirements of the Road Traffic Act.

6.   Make sure you are aware of contractual requirements

In addition to insurances which you must arrange by statute, you may also find yourself asked to have in place, or effect, certain covers as part of a contractual arrangement. These normally relate to Professional Indemnity which, in short, offers cover for financial loss arising out of errors or omissions in your advice.

Such contracts can also ask for Public Liability insurance and, if appropriate, Products Liability insurance.

It is worth noting that these covers are often basic requirements of contracts with local authorities and other public bodies.

7. Consider your Own Risk Profile and Manage Your Risk

Insurers will often allow discounts if you are agreeable to a deductible (or excess) to be applied to your policy. You may also select to self-insure some aspects of your risk and you should discuss the options available to you in depth with your selected broker in establishing your own risk profile.

Insurers will normally reward a well-run business with lower premiums as good housekeeping and good risk management will minimise their potential exposure to claims. Always try to follow your industry's best practice standards and also ensure you comply with the requirements of Health and Safety legislation and guidance. Always do your best to discharge your duty of care to all Third Parties as well as your moral obligation for the safety and well-being of your staff.

8. Budget Yours Costs Correctly

Remember that expenditure in respect of insurance may not limited to the cost of the premium being asked to enable the risk transfer. You should also budget to include the following, as relevant to your particular trade:-

- Fire extinguishing appliances
- Good quality door locks and window locks
- Other physical security, such as bars or grills
- Health & Safety consultancy and implementation
- An intruder alarm
- CCTV

- Staff training
- A fire alarm

9. Review Your Arrangements Regularly

When you have worked with your broker to design a tailor-made insurance programme that matches your needs and budget, do not consider that an end to the matter.

All businesses alter over a period of time maybe by changing their business focus or acquiring extra staff or vehicles. Newer businesses tend to change more frequently and you should therefore make sure your broker is aware of all developments so that he may advise you accordingly.

10. Further Financial Advice

Make sure your insurance broker is able to offer other financial advice which would protect your business or find an Independent Financial Adviser who is skilled in the needs of a business. They should be able to advise you on, for example, insuring important people in your business (Key Man Assurance) and protecting the shareholdings of investors in your business (Share Purchase Assurance). They should also be able to help you out with such things as Pensions and other Employee Benefits, typically Group Life Insurance, Group Private Medical Insurance, Health Insurance and the like.

Gordon Westcott is the Development Manager of Knighthood Corporate Assurance Service plc (Company Registration No. 1194084)

Knighthood is authorised and regulated by the Financial Services Authority (FSA) authorisation Reference 126707.

Appendix 3

Social Media

Top Tips for Start-ups
Social Media - JMC

Back in the mists of time, some forward-thinking individual added a telephone number to his business card. Years later, fax numbers appeared beneath the phone number. Nowadays, it's highly unlikely that you will find a business that doesn't have a website and email contact details. It is also very likely that businesses you encounter will also have links to social media sites. Love it or hate it, social media is very influential and is here to stay. In the United States, 90% of small to medium businesses have a presence in social media. 74% of these perceive that presence as valuable. Those engaged in social media claimed that one quarter of their new customers approached them via this medium. Social media is no longer a playground for university students and bored office workers; it has become an essential business tool.

There are obvious complications with this, and the clue is in the name. Social media was intended to be social. Probably the most well-known example of this medium, Facebook, was initially designed for students to keep in social contact and at its most serious, merely to discuss the location of tonight's party, to display the photos of said party afterwards, or share notes and ideas about their course. Initially, you couldn't even join the network unless you had a valid university email account. But these students grew up, graduated, entered the world of work and realised that this social network they had built up could be used as a business networking forum. Presence in social media began to have a commercial value. The restrictions about joining this network have now been relaxed to such an extent that every man, woman, child or pet can have their own Facebook page so the idea of it being a resource pool of highly educated graduates has passed, but the business potential remains - not only as a recruiting tool but as a new market.

With such a huge market available, it would seem foolish not to try and tap into it. However, the 'social' trap is still there. This medium was designed to be social. Most people using it are trying to socialise. And you want to be sociable too, right? Most people like to share jokes, stories, photos and anecdotes with friends, but potential paying clients may not be so interested. If you want to be sociable, be sociable, and if you want to use this medium for business, be sensible. I know it sounds very patronising to recommend keeping a separate social account from a professional business one, but so very many people don't understand this simple difference. I recommend you take a look around some of the pages on Facebook. At the time of writing this, I came across the page of a photographer with a gallery of high quality portrait work. The same gallery contained personal photos of him looking decidedly compromised and unprofessional. I doubt I'll book him for any shoots in the near future.

If you're going to use social media, keep your social life separate from your business life. This is put into a clearer perspective by Twitter. Constantly uploading 'tweets' about your life, movements and experiences can create the image of a busy professional. It can lead to responses, questions, advice or even potential clients. It can also end careers. Take a look back at the headlines in the red tops over the past few years. Headlines about people who've not understood that a comment intended for like-minded friends is available for anyone with a computer to see. Whether messages written on Twitter should be taken as seriously as formal letters written in print is up for debate.

The use of Twitter seriously divides people. There are many who deride it, thanks to the number of inane comments posted on it. Do people really care which type of banana you had for breakfast, how late your train was running or how long you spent stuck in a lift? Not a lot, I'd imagine. However, there are also those who believe that this personal touch, allowing people an insight into your everyday life, makes you appear more human, normal and therefore approachable. It's very much a sliding scale. Depending on what exactly your business is, your use of Twitter may vary. If you're trying to present yourself as a slick, hard-nosed, serious professional type, posting tweets about your favourite types of biscuit or your preferred brand of breakfast cereal might not help your cause. If, however, you want to create the image of a friendly, trusted, man-of-the-people, nice person who you'd be happy to introduce your granny to, perhaps insights into your personal life via Twitter would be a good way to cultivate that image.

I'd imagine most people are somewhere in-between and can only advise simple common sense on how you use this new medium. Large companies will not tweet about the minutia of life, but breakfast radio DJs will tweet on anything. They want to become your friend, become part of your family morning routine and create a personal attachment to you. That's their job and Twitter is a great medium for it. You need to look at yourself and at your business and find out what fits for you.

LinkedIn is another social media favourite. Often referred to as 'Facebook for grown-ups', you won't find family skiing holiday photos or pets in amusing outfits on here. LinkedIn is probably what Facebook would have become if it had limited its members to graduates. Pages tend to consist of people promoting themselves and their company or showcasing themselves in order to get work elsewhere. And there's the rub. LinkedIn is the third site discussed here and is distinctly different from the first two, which in turn are distinctly different from each other and the many other social media forums available. At the time of writing, Google+ is rapidly encroaching on Facebook and Twitter, numerous rivals have emerged to threaten LinkedIn, and Yahoo are reportedly preparing to take the lead with their own version of social media. The fact of the matter is that there is no golden rule as to which social media site you should market yourself on; you need to do your research and find out which site is right for you, can bring you the right customers and will be worth your while investing your time in.

Far too many websites today have links to nearly every social media site existing. Not only have they failed to discern which sites might bring them any joy, they have overreached themselves and become laden with too many. The average user of Facebook is in their mid-twenties and thus has little interest in purchasing a retirement villa, whilst the members of LinkedIn will have little need for GCSE study guides. Know your market. Know your tools. Know how to use them. Social media can be a game-changing blessing if used properly. If you were to sign up to every social media site, then your website would look very impressive, but you'd be missing the point. The clue is in the name: social.

Social media is two-way. That's what differentiates it from normal media. Unlike an advert in a newspaper that people can read then choose to remember or forget, social media invites a response. People can read what you're offering and then reply. Some may say, 'What a fantastic deal, I really like your company and the way you work,' or 'What a rip-off, do you really expect me to pay that?' to which you can reply 'Thank you. Take a look at our website, there are plenty of other good deals to be had,' or 'What exactly was your problem with our pricing?' (respectively). It's a two-way process. If you don't selectively choose which areas of social media to focus, you'll be hard pressed to respond to all of the comments you receive. Perhaps some people can manage it, but if you sign up to every social media site available and don't follow up on comments, questions and complaints, then you've wasted your time. You may as well have pasted an advert on a lamppost. People want replies. The point of social media is to be social. It is about striking up conversation and discussion. To be honest, if you fail to do this, then you are doing more harm than good to yourself. Constantly tweeting and posting may make you feel good but it's really no different to regularly updating your website. Unless you communicate.

If you have a computer at hand, then look through the choices of type fonts available. Hundreds, probably. There are so many to choose from, but when writing a letter, we select the right tool for the job and use it to get our point across. Social media is out there; it may be changing and evolving but it's not going away any time soon. It has been portrayed as being both a curse and a blessing, but if you pick the right tool and use it wisely then social media could expand your horizons considerably.

A few words about blogs and blogging. This is a good way of establishing you as a subject matter expert and stimulating interaction with others. You can also cross reference your blogs on LinkedIn and Twitter. In terms of workload, you don't have to crank out blogs every day, but one a week would be a good start. Blogs don't have to be long; between 300 and 400 words is sufficient to attract and retain the interest of others, and to be picked up by search engines.

One final aspect concerning personal branding. It is really important that all the sites where you are present in your business capacity convey a consistent and coherent summary of who you are, what you do, what you stand for, etc. Anything else and you run the risk that people cannot make the connection between the carbon-based life form in front of them and the individual they have encountered over the internet - you need to be 100% authentic.

Other Useful Reading

Other Useful Reading

Ashton, R. (2004) *The Entrepreneur's Book of Checklists*, Pearson

Carter, M. (2004) *It's All Cobblers*, Management Books

Essential Business (2008) *The Essential Business Guide*, 3rd edition, Ashford Press

Gerber, M. (2001) *The E-Myth Revisited*, HarperCollins

Lambert, T. (2001) *High Income Consulting*, Nicholas Brealey

Southon, M. and West, C. (2005) *Sales on a Beermat*, Random House

Southon, M. and West, C. (2004) T*he Beermat Entrepreneur*, Random House

Warnes, B. (1994) *The Genghis Khan Guide to Business*, 12th edition, Osmosis

Weiss, A, (2000) *Getting started in Consulting*, Wiley

Williams, S. (2003) *Small Business Guide*, 16th edition, Press Vitesse